W9-BKD-542

Altered Art
for the first time®

Madeline Arendt

Sterling Publishing Co., Inc.
New York
A Sterling/Chapelle Book

Chapelle, Ltd., Inc., P.O. Box 9252, Ogden, UT 84409
(801) 621-2777 • (801) 621-2788 Fax
e-mail: chapelle@chapelleltd.com
Web site: www.chapelleltd.com

Library of Congress Cataloging-in-Publication Data

Arendt, Madeline.
Altered art for the first time / Madeline Arendt.
p. cm.
"A Sterling/Chapelle Book."
Includes bibliographical references and index.
ISBN 1-4027-1655-9
1. Altered books. I. Title.

TT896.3.A74 2005
702'.8'1--dc22

2005010344

10 9 8 7 6 5 4 3 2 1
Published by Sterling Publishing Co., Inc.
387 Park Avenue South, New York, NY 10016
©2005 by Madeline Arendt
Distributed in Canada by Sterling Publishing
% Canadian Manda Group, 165 Dufferin Street
Toronto, Ontario, Canada M6K 3H6
Distributed in Great Britain by Chrysalis Books Group PLC,
The Chrysalis Building, Bramley Road, London W10 6SP, England
Distributed in Australia by Capricorn Link (Australia) Pty. Ltd.
P.O. Box 704, Windsor, NSW 2756, Australia
Printed and Bound in China
All Rights Reserved

Sterling ISBN 1-4027-1655-9

For information about custom editions, special sales, premium
and corporate purchases, please contact Sterling Special Sales
Department at 800-805-5489 or specialsales@sterlingpub.com.

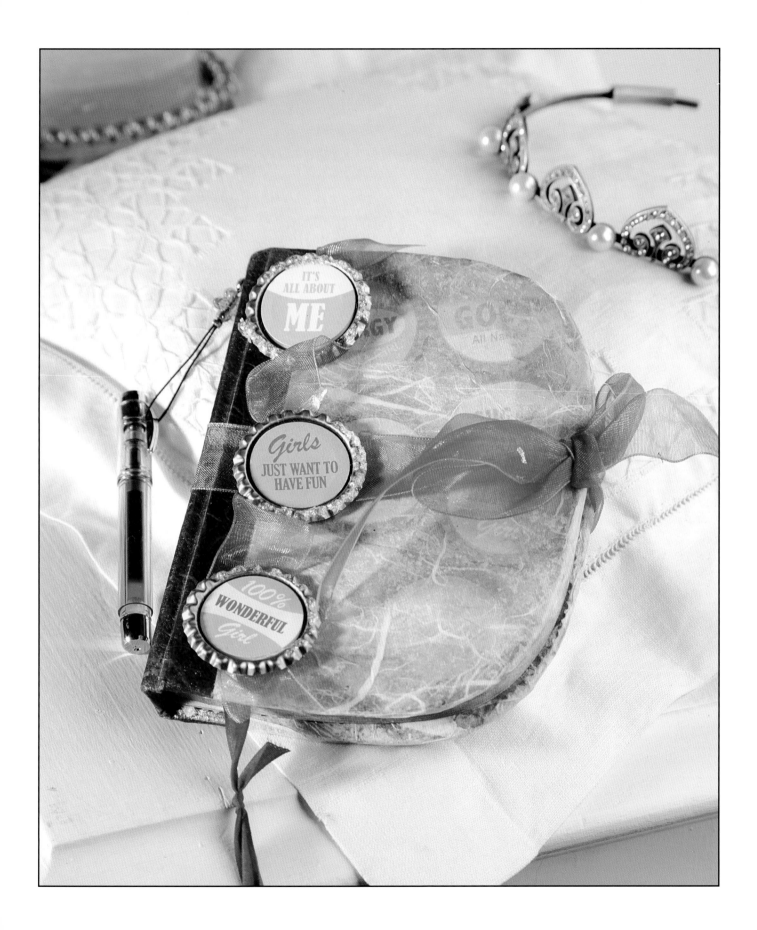

Table of Contents

Section 1:
Altered Art Basics — 10

Section 2:
Basic Projects — 32

Section 3:
Projects Beyond the Basics — 72

Section 4:
Gallery — 96

Introduction

Altered Art can be described as an art form that refashions an object, using a variety of techniques and mediums, giving the object a new purpose or look.

Why would someone want to alter something? My first response would be because it is truly enjoyable to do. Also, it is a way to take unwanted or old items and recycle them into pieces of art. What can be altered? The answer is: anything. The list can be endless. It is only limited to your imagination and your view of things.

Since becoming interested in this art form, I look at everyday objects very differently. You have to look beyond its original purpose. You can create works of art that are beautiful, personal, and useful.

Altering books is not something new. Back in the 11th century, monks in Italy took old manuscripts made from costly parchment and altered the pages by scraping or rubbing off the ink, or covering over the original text. This early form of altering books is called palimpsest. During the Victorian era, people used old books as scrapbooks. Following a trend set by William Granger, they pasted ephemera from their period, which included magazine images, family pictures, and personal recipes onto the pages. This practice of illustrating an old book with items is called "Grangerism." A British artist, Tom Phillips, took a copy of a Victorian novel titled "A Human Document" and altered the pages of the book. He painted over the pages, leaving only a few words showing. The words were used to suggest a painting he would then add to the pages. His creation of a beautiful altered book was called "A Humument." Today, Tom Phillips is widely considered to be the father of modern altered art and altered-art books.

Altered books can be made from old, outdated books, flea-market finds, thrift-store buys, bookstore bargains, rummage sales, and more.

A quick thought on whether using books in this way is considered wrong. Many old books are tossed into the trash or incinerated. Overstocked or outdated books will likely end up the same way. If you think about it this way, you are really saving a book.

The books you choose will become the canvases for your creativity. What you do to the books is your choice. You can glue, cut, paint, punch, sew, drill, wire, collage, stamp, fold, staple, and embellish them. How much or how little you do to the books is your choice. Altered books are created for different reasons. Most are made as a conversational piece. Others are made with a certain theme in mind for a friend or yourself. They can be made into a daily journal, a keepsake of a special occasion, or as a remembrance of something or someone special. They can tell a story. They can become a treasure box or a shrine, or simply a creative piece of art that you will want to display.

There are no rules for this art form. "Anything goes" in altered art. There is not a right or wrong way to make your creations. The materials that can be used are not limited either. The art and craft industries today have so many wonderful products available. Because of the popularity of scrapbooking, most manufacturers are developing products that are acid-free. There also are products available that can be sprayed on papers or pages to help make them archival safe. The altered-art look can be easily incorporated into the craft of scrapbooking as it lends itself well to memory keeping. With this style, the book becomes part of the keepsakes with meaningful photos and memorabilia. Everything that is available for the scrapbooker to use can also be used in altered art.

Truthfully, you could walk the aisles of both fine arts and craft stores and find more than you need in the way of supplies.

When altering a book, do not think it is necessary to do something to each page of the book. When working with large books, you will likely glue blocks of pages together for various reasons. Many of the projects in *Altered Art for the first time* use children's board books. These are easy to use because the pages come already stiffened. Since most of these books have a limited number of pages, you can easily use every page for your art.

To be able to do altered art, you do not have to be an expert in any specific area of the arts. Anyone who likes to create things by hand should enjoy this interesting craft. All altered works reflect each artist's individual taste, style, and ability. Altered art brings together both artists and crafters of all levels, ages, and categories.

Many people are taking part in "round robins." This is the term used to describe a group of people who choose a book, set a theme, and send the book from person to person so each can add their artwork to the pages. This is a good way to get involved in the process of altering. You see the uniqueness that each participant brings to the altered book.

With the availability of computers at home or in public libraries, searching for additional information or altered art groups is relatively easy. As a resource to start with, go the Web site of the International Society of Altered Book Artists, (www.alteredbookartists.com). Another recommendation is the altered book e-group, (http://groups.yahoo.com/group/alteredbooks). You can find information from others interested in altered books. You will find files containing suggestions and how-tos, and photos of other members' works as well as links to other sites.

How to Use this Book

Altered Art for the first time will introduce you to the art of altering a variety of objects. Most of the projects will be using books. For someone trying this form of art for the first time, my hope is to give you the necessary basic information on techniques, supplies, and surfaces to help you create your own wonderful pieces of altered art. Let me repeat this one point again and say that there is nothing you could do wrong when trying your hand at altered art. You cannot make a mistake. If you truly do not like something you did, you can find a way to cover it over.

Section 1: Altered Art Basics familiarizes you with the materials you can use. It provides a guide to the supplies needed and gives an explanation of why you may want to use them and how to use them. It also shows and explains some examples of the basic techniques used.

Section 2: Basic Projects presents pieces that demonstrate how to use a variety of existing books to create works of art, conversational pieces, or keepsakes.

Section 3: Projects Beyond the Basics expands into ideas that use a variety of items to create other unique altered pieces.

Section 4: Gallery will take you beyond books to other surfaces with a host of ideas to show that your creativity is unlimited.

Altered Art for the first time is to be used as a starting point in the process of altering everyday items into works of art. This is an art form where virtually any technique may be tried and combined with another. Products and materials that are used in these projects are my individual choices. If you desire a simpler, cleaner look for your own project, then strive to develop that look. It is not necessary to add large amounts of ephemera and use every technique to make your work special. Once you start, you will soon see how you can manipulate books, pages, and other surfaces to make your own interesting art.

Section 1: Altered Art Basics

What do I need to get started?

Theme

The first thing you will need is a book and/or a theme. This is similar to the famous question, "Which came first, the chicken or the egg?" Which comes first in your creative process will depend on you. If you first have the theme in mind, then you can look for an appropriate book that somehow relates to that theme. If you begin with a book you might have on hand, then you must choose a theme that will suit the book.

Books

Any hardcover book can be used for Altered Art. A wide variety of ready-made books are used in the basic projects section. It is best to avoid glue-bound soft-covered books because this type of book can fall apart quickly.

Children's books are fun to work with. Board books with thick, heavy pages are great books to begin with.

Books with interactive pages, containing puzzle pieces and peek-a-boo windows, can make the artwork interesting. Look for books with odd shapes, then use the shapes to your advantage.

Themed books such as holiday books are great to begin with. Keepsake books for baby or weddings make for another starting point. It is also a good idea to choose a book because the title will fit your theme.

There are other surfaces that can be used for altering beyond the basic book. These surfaces will be outlined in the materials lists for the pieces in the Projects Beyond the Basics section.

Adhesives

In most cases when altering a book or another surface, you will need to use adhesives for holding things together. Some altered-book artists prefer to use only gel mediums.

Quick-dry adhesive
Liquid adhesive
Decoupage glue
Paper adhesive
Sticky dots
Large glue stick
Double-sided tape
Double-sided tape sheets

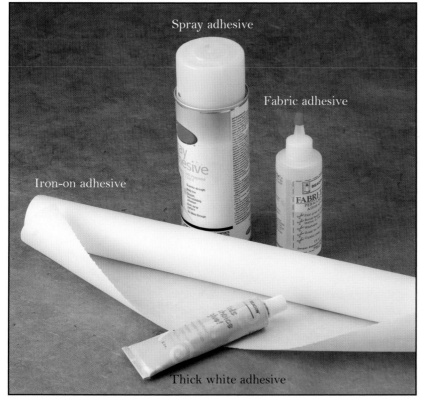

Spray adhesive
Fabric adhesive
Iron-on adhesive
Thick white adhesive

However, there is no rule stating that you must use these. It is really up to you. Use what you have or what you like to work with. The adhesives you choose to use can be varied. In most cases, it will depend on what you are applying and to what type of surface you are adhering it. The adhesives suggested for the completion of projects in this book have all been tested. They work well in each case for which they have been used.

In a regular hardcover book with paper pages, a good large glue stick can be used for gluing a few pages together. For applying paper, such as in collage, decoupage glue can be used as well as liquid adhesive. There are a number of paper-specific glues available. In the majority of projects in this book, pages and papers were glued together using a paper adhesive or a quick-dry adhesive. Double-sided tapes and sheets will be used for specific reasons. Glue alternatives such as sticky dots could be helpful in certain situations. When it comes to adding embellishments, a good, thick, white adhesive will work well. If working with fabrics, fabric adhesives are good to have on hand. Another adhesive to use with fabrics is an iron-on adhesive. A can of spray adhesive is also useful in some circumstances, as is the using of a sticker maker for applying adhesive onto certain surfaces.

Paints

If you chose to start with the book as a blank canvas, you may want to prime the pages or sections with paint. If you are using a board book, a white or black flat-finish spray paint can be used to cover the surface of the book. Gesso, either white or black, can be used on the pages, if that's what is preferred. Remember, it is okay to have the original page of the

Flat-finish spray paint

Flat-finish spray paint

Gesso

Flow medium

Light body
opaque acrylics

Light
body
metallic
acrylic

Metallic acrylic

Dimensional paper paint

book show through. The look you want to achieve is all up to you.

Once the pages are primed, other paints can be added. Acrylic paints can be used for this purpose. Light body opaque and metallic or pearlescent acrylic paints are a good start, plus regular metallic acrylics. Other paper-specific products like dimensional paper paints can be used. They can be thinned using either a flow medium or water, then used as glazes, if desired. The metallic acrylic paints also can be used as dimensional paints. Paints can be brushed or sponged on.

Use what you have or like to work with, and feel free to experiment. There also are other products available, specifically for paper arts, that can be used.

Finishes

There are a variety of products that can be used to give a final coat to your projects. Which finish you choose will depend on the original surface or how the

Spray finish

Spray glaze

Brush-on finish
decoupage glue

completed piece will be used. Spray finishes like a clear acrylic are always a good way to protect a finished piece. The choice of a gloss or matte look is the artist's decision. Brush-on finishes also can be used. They come in gloss or matte. Some decoupage glues not only act as adhesives, they also act as finishes and give you an instant aged look with a sepia or antique tone.

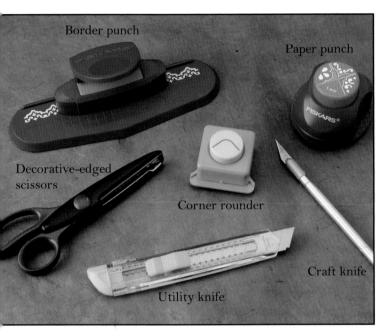

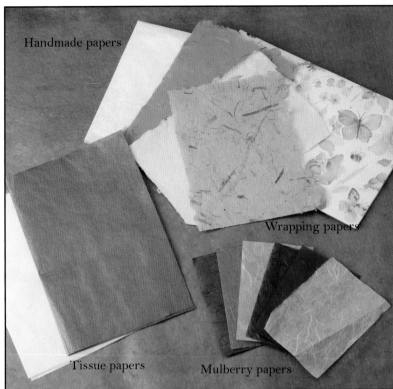

Cutting Tools

The most important tool you will use will be a craft knife with a supply of sharp blades. If thick covers must be cut to change the shape or if you need to cut niches into glued pages, a good heavy-duty utility knife also will be useful.

Decorative paper punches can be used to punch shapes into pages for interesting additions. Decorative-edged scissors and border punches can be used to edge pages or papers.

Papers

Papers of all types can be used in this art form. Some papers that can be used are wrapping papers, scrapbooking papers, mulberry papers, magazine or newspaper clippings, old cards, and pieces torn from old books. Any scraps of paper can be recycled.

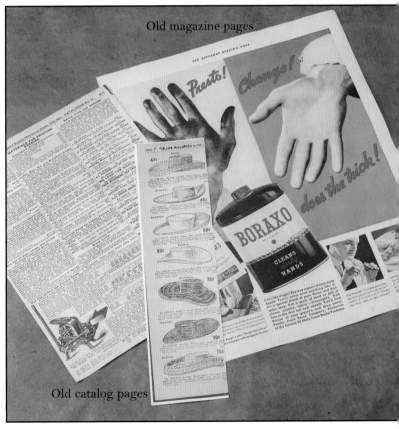

Tissue paper can be used to give texture to pages by scrunching it or allowing it to bunch up or overlap. It also can be used to give the pages a muted look. This is done by covering a completed page or book cover with a single sheet of tissue paper.

Other Tools & Materials

The items in the following list will be necessary or helpful to have on hand.

- **Eyelets & eyelet-setting tools**—for placement in corners of pages to hold large sections together
- **Paper brads**—for holding pages together without gluing or for attaching something to a page
- **Rubber stamps**—for stamping designs onto pages
- **Ink pads**—for aging pages (distress inks) or stamping images (archival inks)
- **Metallic leafing pens**—for edging pages
- **Glitter glue**—for adding sparkling accents to various embellishments
- **Binder clips**—for holding sections of pages together when gluing
- **Spring clamps**—for holding blocks of pages together for gluing
- **Waxed paper**—for placing between pages when gluing
- **Brayer**—for rolling over the pages to smooth when gluing

Glitter glue

Rubber stamps

Ink pads

Eyelet setting tools

Paper brads

Eyelets

Metallic leafing pens

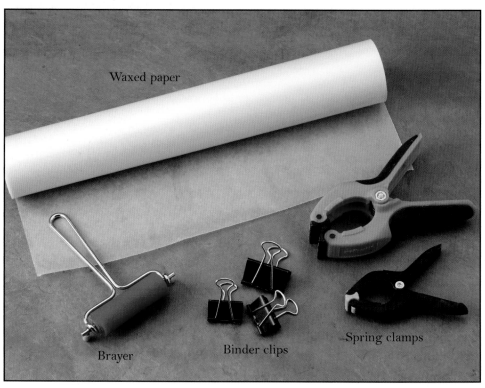

Waxed paper

Brayer

Binder clips

Spring clamps

- **Bone folder**—for creasing papers
- **Hole punch**—for making holes in pages for lacing ribbons, fibers, wire, etc.
- **Metal or metal-edged ruler**—for cutting niches into pages or covers
- **Cutting mat**—for placing under or between pages that will be cut
- **Latex gloves**—for keeping hands clean
- **Paintbrushes (a variety of sizes)**—for applying paints and finishes
- **Cosmetic sponges**—for applying paints or inks to surfaces
- **Brush applicator (a screw-on top, with a large brush)**—for applying liquid adhesive
- **Craft iron**—for ironing on fabric adhesive
- **Sticker maker**—for applying adhesive onto vellum papers for embellishing
- **Sandpaper**—for roughening the smooth surface of board books before painting, for distressing photos or pictures, and for cleaning up cut edges of niches
- **Paper sealer (optional)**—to help prevent warping of color copies, photos, and other papers used

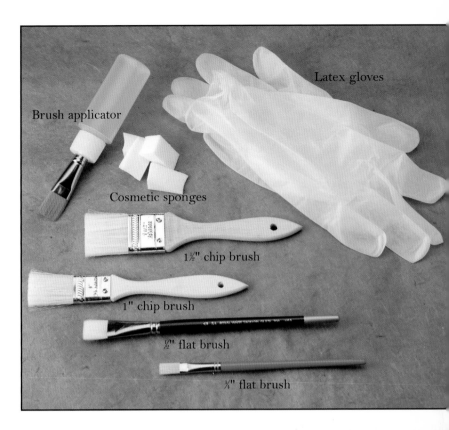

Brush applicator

Latex gloves

Cosmetic sponges

1½" chip brush

1" chip brush

½" flat brush

¼" flat brush

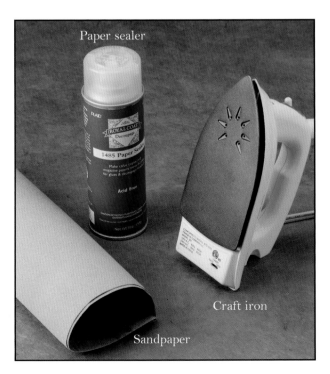

Paper sealer

Craft iron

Sandpaper

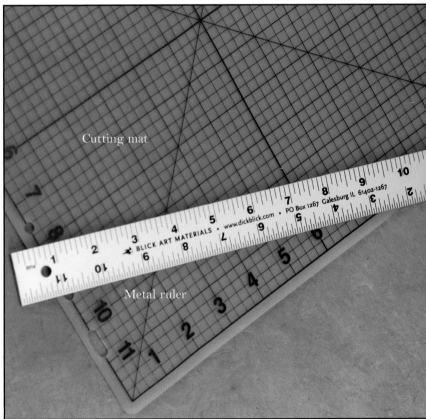

Cutting mat

Metal ruler

Ephemera

This is the best part of altered art. Ephemera will be the touch that gives any of your pieces uniqueness. It's like the icing on the cake. This can truly be an endless list. The following list is only a sampling of what can be used to embellish your works of art. Of course, what you add should relate to the theme with which you are working.

- **Beads**
- **Buttons**
- **Charms**
- **Clay reliefs**
- **Clipart**
- **Decorative clips**
- **Envelopes**
- **Fabric pieces**
- **Fibers**
- **Foam shapes**
- **Keys**
- **Letters, metal/wood/foam**
- **Mini frames**
- **Old jewelry**
- **Paper doilies**
- **Page pebbles**
- **Photo corners**
- **Photos**
- **Postcards**
- **Puzzle pieces**
- **Ribbon**
- **Seashells**
- **Stickers**
- **Tags**
- **Threads**
- **Wooden shapes**

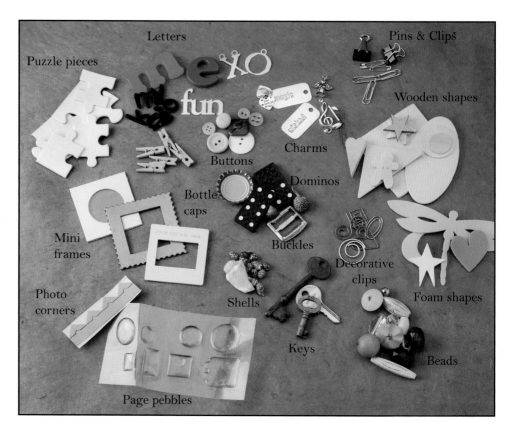

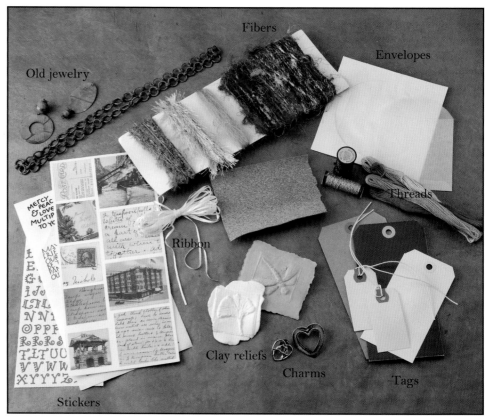

Paper doilies

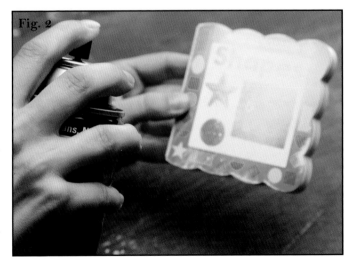

Postcards

Photos

How do I prepare the covers?

Most projects will begin with a book. Whether it is new or used, it may need some prep work. If starting with a new book made from thick board with a slick surface, it would be best to prepare it for painting or collage. The steps are easy.

Fig. 1

Begin sanding the surface of the book with a medium-grit sandpaper. (See Fig. 1) *Note: This will remove some of the slickness, giving the surface some "tooth" to hold paint, glue, and papers.*

Fig. 2

After sanding, spray with a white or black flat-finish

paint before proceeding. (See Fig. 2) *Notes: Whether you use white or black depends on the colors you will be applying over the surface. For example, you wouldn't want to apply light pastel papers or fabrics over a black painted surface. When using spray paints, follow the manufacturer's directions for application and drying time. Some surfaces may need two coats.*

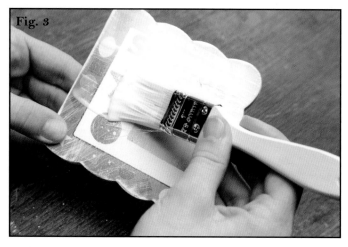

If you do not want use spray paints, brush on any solid acrylic paint. (See Fig. 3)

Should I embellish the cover before beginning the inside?

It is best to prepare and embellish the inside of the book before completing the cover. Most covers will feature three-dimensional pieces that could get ruined during the process of embellishing the inside if they were placed on the book beforehand.

How do I remove pages from inside the book?

Decide whether you will be removing pages. Removing pages will alleviate bulk if you are adding

niches and pockets or adding three-dimensional objects and ephemera.

Usually, pages are removed small sections at a time. Tear out the pages by hand or cut them out with a craft knife. (See Figs. 4–5)

How do I glue pages together?

You will want to glue a number of pages together if you plan on cutting niches for dimensional additions or making pockets. When gluing only a small number of pages together, you can use a glue stick.

When working with board books, use a thick white adhesive or spray adhesive to hold pages together.

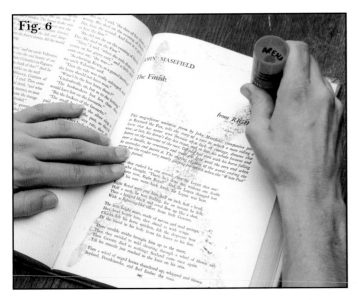
Fig. 6

Beginning at the back of the section, run the glue stick along the edges of the page, then draw a large X in the center of the page. (See Fig. 6) Press the preceding page onto the glued page.

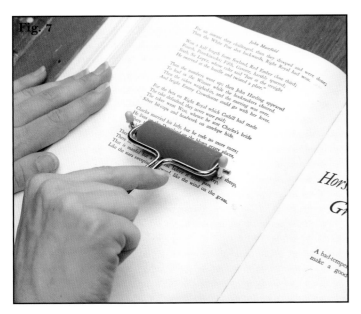
Fig. 7

Rub together by hand or use a brayer. (See Fig. 7)

Continue in this fashion until desired number of pages are glued together. If they begin to buckle, weight the closed book and set aside overnight. *Note: It is sometimes difficult to avoid some buckling.*

How do I glue a block of pages together?

When making niches, you will want to glue enough pages together to form a block, to fit the objects to be placed inside.

Fig. 8

Hold the block of pages together and clamp. (See Fig. 8)

Fig. 9

Using a clear liquid paper adhesive, spread glue over the edges of the clamped pages. (See Fig. 9)

Fig. 10

Use your fingers to spread the glue well, pushing it into the edges. (See Fig. 10)

Fig. 11

Clamp the the glued area with binder clips and set the book aside until dry. (See Fig. 11)

How can I attach pages without using glue?

Pages can be attached by using strings, ribbons, or other fibers. They also can be stapled together.

Thick sections can be wired together. First, drill or punch holes into the corners of the block of pages. (See Figs. 12–13)

Fig. 12

Fig. 13

Fig. 14

Thread wire through the holes and twist closed. (See Fig. 14)

Fig. 15

When using wire, add eyelets to the top and bottom pages to keep the wire from tearing through the pages. (See Fig. 15)

Fig. 16

Fasten a thinner section together by lacing wire, string, ribbon, or fiber through the holes. (See Fig. 16)

Fig. 17

Use paper brads to hold thinner sections together. (See Fig. 17) You may even decide to sew a number of pages together with a needle and thread.

How do I fold or tear pages to create pockets?

Pages can be folded or torn to create interesting visual effects and to prepare for placing a pocket in the book.

Fig. 18

Fold a number of pages over diagonally, pulling them from the top outside corner to the inside of the book. (See Fig. 18)

Fig. 19

Fold pages vertically by pulling them from the outside edge to the inside of the book at different intervals. (See Fig. 19)

Fig. 20

If a torn uneven look is desired, tear two to four pages freehand or with a deckle-edged ruler. (See Fig. 20)

Fig. 21

Punch holes through both the folded pages and a small glued section of pages immediately behind them. (See Fig. 21)

Fig. 22

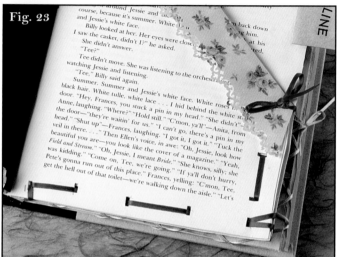

Fig. 23

Fig. 24

Join the pages, using paper brads, ribbons or cords, eyelets, or staples. (See Figs. 22–24)

How do I add pockets for tags?

Hidden pockets can be made specifically for holding a certain size of tag by folding and gluing together the pages in the book or by inserting a folded piece of cardstock.

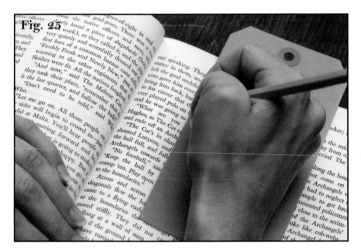

To make a pocket, using only the pages of the book, mark the placement of the pocket on the page by drawing a line about ½" from the edge of the tag to be used. (See Fig. 25)

Apply glue to the outside edge of the page. Continue around the three sides of the tag placement. Spread the glue as needed with your finger. (See Fig. 26)

Lay the preceding page over the glued page and smooth them together. (See Fig. 27)

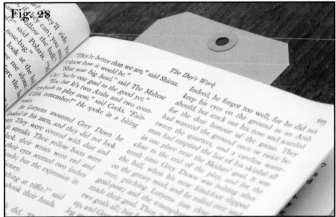

Insert the tag. (See Fig. 28)

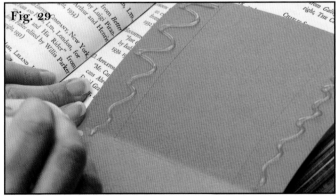

To make a pocket for tags with cardstock, cut a folded piece of cardstock to fit tag. Open and run a bead of glue along side edges of cardstock. Refold cardstock. (See Fig. 29)

Fig. 30

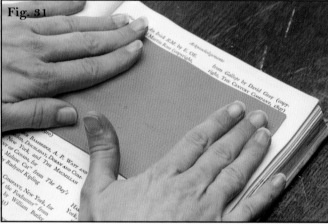
Fig. 31

Run a bead of glue around the edges of the folded cardstock pocket. (See Fig. 30) Place the cardstock pocket, glue side down, onto the page with the top of the pocket along the top edge of the page. (See Fig. 31)

Run a bead of glue around the three sides of the page and on the top side of the cardstock pocket, spreading the glue with your finger as needed.

Lay the preceding page over the glued page and smooth them together.

How do I cut niches, windows, or doors?

A niche is a hole cut through many pages of the book. It gives you a space to place something that you want to stand out. Basically, that will be the reason for making windows or doors, too.

To make a niche, you will have to glue a block of pages together to the thickness of the object that will be placed inside it. Once the thickness is decided, begin gluing the block of pages as directed in **"How do I glue a block of pages together?"** on pages 21–22.

Fig. 32

When the glue is dry, use a pencil and ruler or a template to mark the outline for the niche on the top page of the block. (See Fig. 32) *Note: Square or rectangular niches are easier to cut out than other shapes, but other shapes can add interest to the work.*

Fig. 33

Using a craft knife, start slicing through the pages—begin on one side and continue around. When cutting straight lines, use a metal-edged ruler to help keep the cut edges straight. (See Fig. 33)

Fig. 34

Begin removing the sections that are cut. (See Fig. 34)

Fig. 35

Repeat the cutting and removing process until the desired depth is achieved. (See Fig. 35)

The same process is used when cutting other shapes. Go slowly, through the layers of pages. If the blade gets dull, change to a new sharp blade.

Doors and windows are made in a manner similar to how niches are done, except that they usually are not as deep or large.

If you are adding doors or windows, decide where they will be and if they will be shallow or deep. The size or shape will be determined by what is seen through the window or door.

Fig. 36

For a window, mark the top edge of the window with a pencil on the top page. (See Fig. 36) *Note: It is best not to place them too close to the edge of the page—leave about a ¾" border near the edges of the pages.*

Fig. 37

Mark along the bottom edge of the window in the same manner. (See Fig. 37)

Finally, mark the midpoint, or the point where the two window flaps will open, joining the top and bottom.

Using a craft knife, cut through to the desired depth. (See Fig. 38)

Fig. 38

Note: Always use a cutting mat under the section of pages that will be cut to avoid cutting pages behind the window.

Fig. 39

To create the look of a pane of glass on the opening for a window, adhere a piece of acetate onto the top page, enclosing the object. (See Fig. 39)

Fig. 40

For doors, mark and cut through the two or three sides that will make up the door, leaving one side to act as the hinge. (See Fig. 40) *Note: When making a door for an opening, the easiest way is to fashion the door from a heavier paper, then glue it over the opening.*

Fig. 41

Make certain to allow an entire page to serve as a background for the window or the door. This will be where you place the item to be seen through the window or door. Decorative paper or fabric can be glued onto this page, or it can be painted. (See Fig. 41)

How do I add paint to the pages or covers?

When applying paint to surfaces, the choice is yours. Again, the way the paint is applied is determined by the look you want to achieve. Sponging on the paint is the easiest method of application.

Fig. 42

Place paint onto any type of palette and dip the sponge into the paint. (See Fig. 42)

Fig. 43

Dab the sponge onto the surface of the page or cover. Continue in this manner until the desired effect is achieved. (See Fig. 43)

Fig. 44

Add another color or colors of paint in the same manner, layering and blending colors as desired. (See Fig. 44)

Fig. 45

Stippling is another way to apply paint. Start with paint on a palette, dip the brush into the paint, then dab off excess paint on the side of the palette. With an up-and-down motion, tap the brush onto the surface. (See Fig. 45)

How can I use rubber stamps and ink pads?

To give pages a distressed, aged look, use distress inks and archival inks.

Fig. 46

Fig. 47

Dab one end of a cosmetic sponge onto the ink pad. Apply ink onto the edges of pages or other images by rubbing ink around the edges with the sponge. (See Figs. 46–47)

Fig. 48

printed and handmade papers. You will find that most altered art is based on collage.

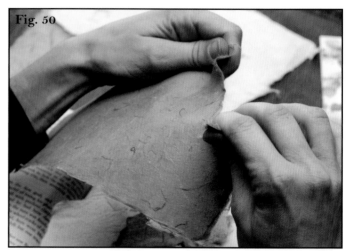
Fig. 50

To create another effect, ink also can be applied using the stippling technique with a flat brush. (See Fig. 48) *Note: This is a technique that you may want to experiment with before using it on your book.*

Use archival inks with rubber stamps to stamp images or verses either directly onto pages or onto other papers that can then be collaged onto the book pages or covers.

Fig. 51
Fig. 52

Fig. 49

Press the stamp into the ink so the image is covered. Press the image onto the paper. (See Fig. 49)

Fig. 53

How do I collage?

The art of collage is a wonderful way to add texture to your creations. Basically, collage is the process of combining and layering relatively flat items—mainly

Start by tearing pieces of paper and cutting out small design elements. (See Figs. 50–51) Arrange the papers in an attractive manner on a page. (See Fig. 52–53)

Fig. 54

Fig. 55

Adhere the pieces onto the surface of the page or cover. Use either the liquid laminating adhesive or a decoupage glue to apply the pieces. (See Figs. 54–55)

Fig. 56

Set aside to dry. (See Fig. 56) Once a background is achieved, embellishments can be added.

How do I embellish my work?

Embellishing with ephemera is the last thing you do, either to a page or cover. This is like putting the icing on a cake. Embellishments are usually dimensional.

Embellishments will add texture and interest to your work. You are really just adding to the collage when adding the embellishments.

Fig. 57

Fig. 58

Use items that relate to the theme of the page or book. When you find the right position for them, glue them in place and allow to dry. (See Figs. 57–58)

"It is through the miracle of love that we discover the fullness of life"

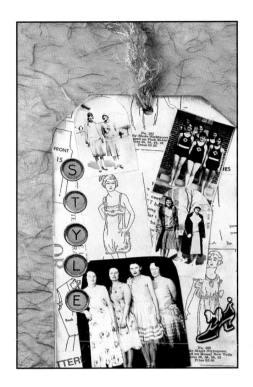

Since the beginning
Girls have wanted
To have FUN!

Section 2: Basic Projects

WYNKEN, BLYNKEN, AND NOD
EUGENE FIELD

PRECIOUS (presh´-es) 1. of great worth
2. beloved; cherished

MIRACLE (mir´-e-kel) 1. an event
or action unexplained by scientific
law 2. an awesome or unimaginable
outcome

BEAUTIFUL (byoot´-e-ful) 1. pleasingly
attractive physical appearance 2. lovely;
fine to behold 3. delicate and favorable

Wynken, Blynken and Nod,
Sailed off in a wooden shoe—
Sailed on a river of crystal light,
Into a sea of dew.
"Where are you going,
and what do you wish?"
The old man asked the three.
"We have come to fish for
the herring fish
That live in this beautiful sea;
Nets of silver and gold have we!"
Said Wynken, Blynken and Nod.

TEN FINGERS

One, two, three, four, fiv
Once I caught a fish alive
Six, seven, eight, nine, ten
But I let him go again.
Why did you let him go?
Because he bit my finger so.
Which finger did he bite?
little one upon the right.

God made the world with its towering trees,
majestic mountains and restless seas.
Then paused and said,
" "It needs one more thing,
someone to laugh and dance and sing.
To walk in the woods and gather flowers."

So God made little girls,

BABY! MY BABY
You're such a sweet wonder, and daily surprise;
With glimpses of heaven, I catch from your eyes.
Through beautiful blue, that you brought from the
skies,   Baby!   My baby!

CURLY
LOCKS

Curly locks! curly locks!
wilt thou be mine?
Thou shalt not wash dishes,
nor yet feed the swine;
But sit on a cushi
a fir

33

1
project

What you need to get started:

Materials
- Flip board book

Adhesives
- Paper adhesive
- Spray adhesive

Ephemera
- Alphabet stickers
- Computer-generated words, definitions
- Lace
- Photo corners
- Ribbon

Paints
- Black light body opaque acrylic paint
- Pearl white light body pearlescent acrylic paint

Papers
- Decorative paper
- Vellum paper

Tools & Other Supplies
- Black soot distress ink pad
- Silver-leafing pen
- Sponge

How do I make a book with paint, computer-generated words, and embellishments?

This is a simple beginning project. It begins with sponge-painting the pages of a small board book. Words and their definitions—describing the person the book is for—are computer generated and printed onto vellum. Decorative paper is used on the covers with a few embellishments.

Word games

Divided pages make for a unique and entertaining book where you can mix and match words and their definitions.

Define Yourself

Here's how:

1. Refer to **How do I prepare the covers?** on pages 19–20. Prepare front and back covers.

2. Refer to **How do I add paint to the pages or covers?** on pages 28–29. Sponge each page of the book with paints.

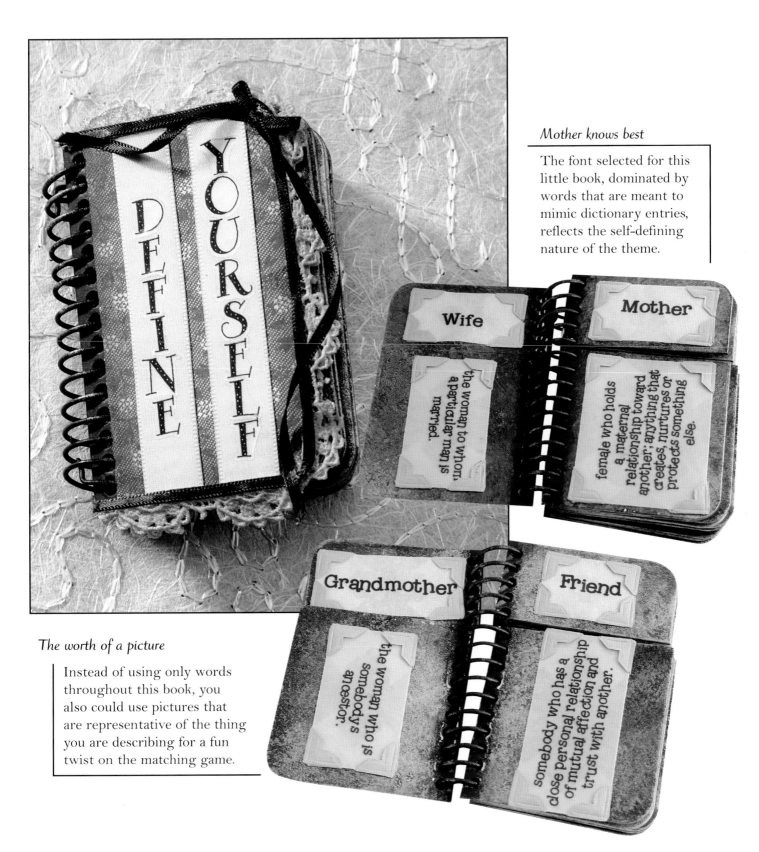

The font selected for this little book, dominated by words that are meant to mimic dictionary entries, reflects the self-defining nature of the theme.

DEFINE YOURSELF

Wife

the woman to whom a particular man is married.

Mother

female who holds a maternal relationship toward another; anything that creates, nurtures or protects something else.

Grandmother

the woman who is somebody's ancestor.

Friend

somebody who has a close personal relationship of mutual affection and trust with another.

The worth of a picture

Instead of using only words throughout this book, you also could use pictures that are representative of the thing you are describing for a fun twist on the matching game.

35

3. Apply spray adhesive onto the back of decorative paper, then adhere onto both front and back covers of the book—inside and out.

4. Attach words and definitions onto pages with photo corners.

5. Adhere ribbon and alphabet stickers onto cover as desired.

Woman

an adult female human being; feminine qualities or feelings.

Teacher

somebody who teaches, especially as a profession; anything from which something may be learned.

Creative

good at a form of creative expression; skill and showing taste, able to imagination; able to appreciate the beauty and worth of art.

6. Color lace by rubbing ink onto lace with a sponge.

7. Adhere lace onto edge of cover.

8. Adhere ribbon and bow onto top of cover.

How do I make a book by altering only the cover and embellishing the pages?

Small, themed gift books found in bookstores and gift shops can easily be slightly altered to make something special. Cover the outside of the book with a coordinating decorative paper. Add ribbons and bow to make it look like a gift package.

What you need to get started:

Materials
• Inspiration book

Adhesives
• Fabric adhesive
• Sheet of double-sided tape
• Thick white adhesive

Ephemera
• Buttons
• Decorative clips
• Glitter
• Jewels
• Ribbon
• Sticker with friendship verse
• Tag
• Tiny paper brads

Paints
• Dimensional paints: various colors

Papers
• Decorative paper for covers
• Decorative paper for inside covers

Tools & Other Supplies
• Craft scissors

Just for you

Gift books are nice to work with because there are short verses and simple pictures that are relatively easy to alter.

Wrapped in Ribbons *(Photos on pages 38–39)*

Here's how:

1. Refer to **How do I prepare the covers?** on pages 19–20. Prepare front and back covers.

2. Apply decorative paper for front and back covers onto sheet of double-sided tape, then adhere onto covers.

37

3. Cut ribbon into strips to fit front cover. Adhere ribbon strips onto cover with fabric adhesive.

4. Cut pieces of decorative paper to fit inside front and back covers, then glue in place with thick white adhesive.

5. Embellish each page as desired, with brads, buttons, decorative clips, dimensional paints, glitter, jewels, ribbon, and stickers, to follow theme.

6. Add bow.

7. Tie on a tag with title.

is a single soul dwelling in two bodies

Love

Aristotle

3
project

What you need to get started:

Materials
- Blank journal

Adhesives
- Glitter glue
- Liquid adhesive

Ephemera
- Bottle caps
- Decorative bead, button, or charm
- Ribbons
- Stickers

Papers
- Decorative papers
- Mulberry paper
- White tissue paper

Other Tools & Supplies
- Craft scissors
- Fired brick distress ink pad
- Paintbrush
- Small pen
- Sponge
- Waxed thread

How do I make a daily diary with collage and embellishing?

An inexpensive, purse-sized, blank diary becomes even more personal by covering the outside with any variety of papers in a favorite color. Embellish it with monograms or other trinkets.

Style matters

A lined notebook like this one is compact and fashionable—the perfect accessory for your purse.

Girl's Diary

Here's how:

1. Refer to **How do I prepare the covers?** on pages 19–20. Prepare front and back covers.

2. Refer to **How do I collage?** on pages 30–31. Collage pieces of decorative paper onto both outside and inside of front and back covers. Begin with a decorative paper, layering tissue paper on top. Allow papers to dry.

3. Refer to **How can I use rubber stamps and ink pads?** on pages 29–30. Apply ink onto the outside edges of the inside pages.

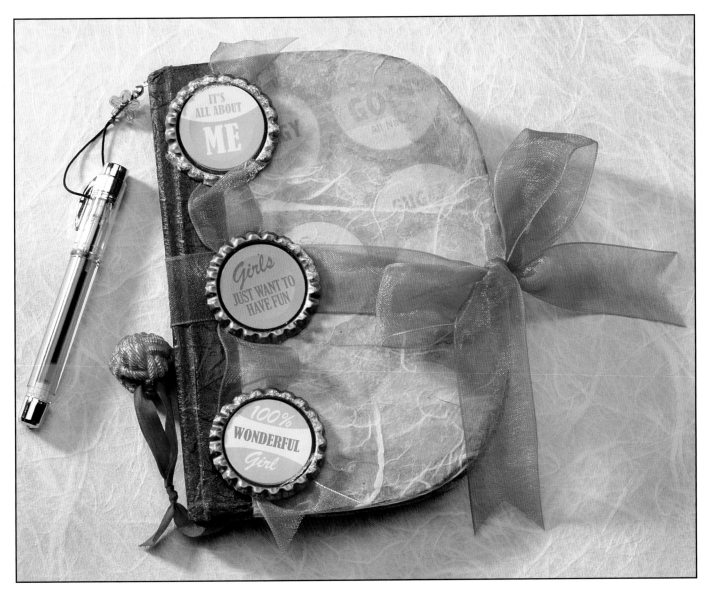

4. Adhere a length of ribbon onto the inside back cover to act as a page marker. Add decorative bead, button, or charm to the ribbon.

5. Cut a piece of mulberry paper large enough to cover the spine. Adhere the paper onto the spine with liquid adhesive.

6. Attach a length of ribbon for a tie closure.

7. Adhere bottle caps and appropriate stickers onto the cover.

8. Brush edges of bottle caps with glitter glue.

9. Attach a small pen to the spine with waxed thread.

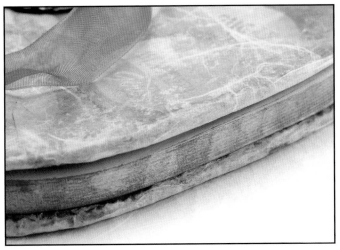

How do I make a keepsake book from a blank sketchbook?

What you need to get started:

Materials

- Blank cloth-covered sketchbook

Adhesives

- Double-sided ½" tape
- Paper adhesive

Ephemera

- Buttons
- Color-copied images
- Decorative ribbon
- Jute cord
- Number stickers
- Photo corners
- Star clips

Paints

- Gold light body metallic acrylic paint
- Light body opaque acrylic paints: blue; red

Papers

- Decorative papers

Tools & Other Supplies

- ⅛" circle hole punch
- Alphabet rubber stamps
- Jet black or sepia archival ink pad
- Sponge

Wanting to create a clever way to hold memories from my grandson's first year of school, I found the blank sketchbook to be a fabulous solution. Each new year another journal can be added to hold special photos or papers.

Arts and crafts

This particular sketchbook, purchased at an arts supplies store, is covered with fabric that is easy to paint. The blank inside pages lend themselves to endless decorating possibilities

Kindergarten Keepsake

Here's how:

1. Refer to **How do I add paint to the pages or covers?** on pages 28–29. Sponge the front and back covers with paints.

2. Divide the inside pages into sections. Refer to **How do I fold or tear pages to create pockets?** on pages 23–24. In each section, diagonally fold four or five pages together to form the front of a pocket.

3. Glue the next four or five pages together to form the back of the pocket.

4. Tear strips of decorative papers the height of the pages, making them wide enough to fold over the edges of the glued sections.

5. Adhere the strips along the edges of each glued section with paper adhesive.

6. Evenly punch holes along bottom of pockets and up each side to the edge of the fold.

7. Lace jute cord through the holes and tie into bow at the edge of the pocket.

8. Stamp the names of the months along the folded edge of the pockets.

9. Adhere ribbons, buttons, clips, stickers, and images onto the cover.

How do I make an interactive holiday book?

Small board books with doors that lift can become a book filled with surprises. Choose a theme and decorate the book accordingly. Under each door, place something that represents your theme.

Open and shut

A book with built-in doors provides places for hiding art elements—no need to cut the pages yourself.

Winter Snow *(Photos on pages 46–47)*

Here's how:

1. Refer to **How do I prepare the covers?** on pages 19–20. Prepare front and back covers.

2. Using sticker maker, apply adhesive to the back of textured paper, then adhere the textured paper onto the front and back covers.

3. Refer to **How do I add paint to the pages or covers?** on pages 28–29. Sponge the pages with white paint, then finish with white pearl paint.

What you need to get started:

Materials
- Peek-a-boo board book

Adhesives
- Glitter glue
- Double-sided 1" tape
- Thick white adhesive

Ephemera
- Charms
- Iridescent cord
- Metal alphabet letters
- Sequins
- Snowflake buttons
- Stickers
- White ribbon

Paints
- Blue sapphire dimensional paint
- Textured snow paint
- White acrylic paint
- White pearl acrylic paint

Papers
- Vellum or clear verse stickers
- White textured paper

Tools & Other Supplies
- ⅛" circle hole punch
- 24-gauge white wire
- Flat brush
- Silver-leafing pen
- Sponge
- Sticker maker

45

4. Using flat brush, stipple the hidden area under the doors with blue sapphire paint.

5. Paint the doors with the textured snow paint. Allow to dry.

6. Using sticker maker, apply adhesive to the back of vellum verses, then adhere the verses onto the pages.

7. Punch holes and tie a piece of iridescent cord onto each door.

8. Adhere verse-related ephemera under each door with thick white adhesive.

9. Attach metal letters to wire and adhere them onto the cover. Add snowflake buttons and other ephemera.

10. Adhere ribbon onto the cover with double-sided tape.

11. Using the silver leafing pen, color the edges of all pages and doors.

12. Use your finger to spread glitter glue around the edges of the verses.

Winter wonderland

Layered metallic snowflakes hidden behind one of the interactive doors seem to pop off the page right into your hands.

6
project

What you need to get started:

Materials
- Composition book

Adhesives
- Antique decoupage glue
- Iron-on fabric adhesive
- Thick white adhesive

Ephemera
- Alphabet stickers
- Belt
- Lace pieces
- Old glasses
- Tag

Tools & Other Supplies
- 24-gauge copper wire
- Burlap and homespun fabric
- Craft Iron

How do I make a journal from a composition book?

An ordinary black-and-white composition book can be transformed into a personal journal for writing down ideas or thoughts. An old pair of reading glasses is used on the cover to make it extraordinary.

Cover up

The simple surface of this composition book practically begs to be covered with fabrics, decorative papers, and paints.

Look Into Yourself

Here's how:

1. Measure fabric to cover from the inside front to the inside back cover. Cut fabric to fit composition book.

2. Apply iron-on fabric adhesive to the fabric or burlap, following manufacturer's directions.

3. Iron the fabric onto the composition book, wrapping the ends to the inside of the front and back covers.

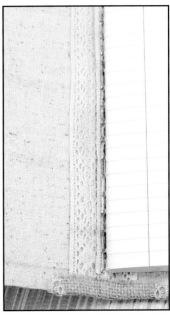

4. Trim top and bottom edges if necessary.

5. Apply burlap onto spine in same manner, following Steps 2–4.

6. Adhere torn papers and lace scraps onto cover with decoupage glue.

7. Attach belt onto back cover with wire.

8. Embellish with ephemera as desired.

7

project

What you need to get started:

Materials
- Mini board book

Adhesives
- Double-sided ⅛" tape
- Liquid adhesive
- Paper adhesive

Ephemera
- Eyelets
- Ribbon
- Stickers
- Tiny tags
- Wired cord

Papers
- Coordinating solids
- Decorative papers
- Tiny envelopes

Tools & Other Supplies
- ⅛" circle hole punch
- Bone folder
- Distress ink pads
- Eyelet-setting tools
- Gold metallic pen

How do I work with a mini board book?

Most small board books have only a few pages, making them the perfect starting place for a "Star Book." Besides a "stars and stripes" theme, think about those special "stars" in your life for whom a book could be made.

Sweet and simple

Because this book is so small, the process of altering it can be completed in one session at your crafting table.

America

Here's how:

1. Refer to **How do I prepare the covers?** on pages 19–20. Prepare front and back covers.

2. Refer to **How do I collage?** on page 30–31. Collage pieces of decorative papers onto the front and back covers.

3. Center and punch one hole into each cover along outer edges. Apply eyelets to both holes.

4. Measure pages. Cut paper strips to equal the height of the pages but ½"–1" shorter than the width of the two pages when the book is open. Cut another contrasting paper into strips the same height, but ½" shorter than the first.

5. Fold each piece in half, creasing with a bone folder.

6. Apply double-sided tape along the edges of each larger strip.

7. Before removing the tape backing, find the strip's placement inside the book. Mark with a pencil. Remove the backing and adhere the paper strip into the book. Continue with remaining larger strips.

8. Apply contrasting smaller strips in the same fashion as for the larger strips, following Steps 5–7.

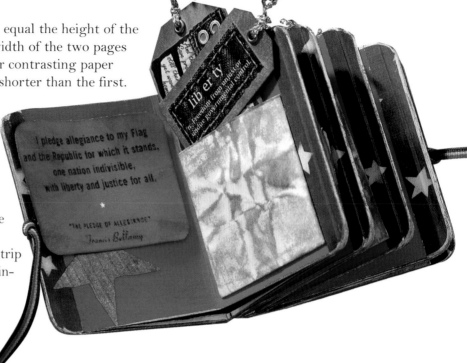

9. Refer to **How can I use rubber stamps and ink pads?** on pages 29–30. Distress tiny envelopes by scrunching them and adding inks.

10. Glue tiny envelopes onto the pages.

11. Adhere stickers to tiny tags. Age tags with distress inks.

12. Add wired cord to tags. Place tags into envelope pockets.

13. Tie ribbon through the eyelets on the covers.

14. Color the edges of the pages with metallic pen.

15. Embellish cover with ephemera as desired.

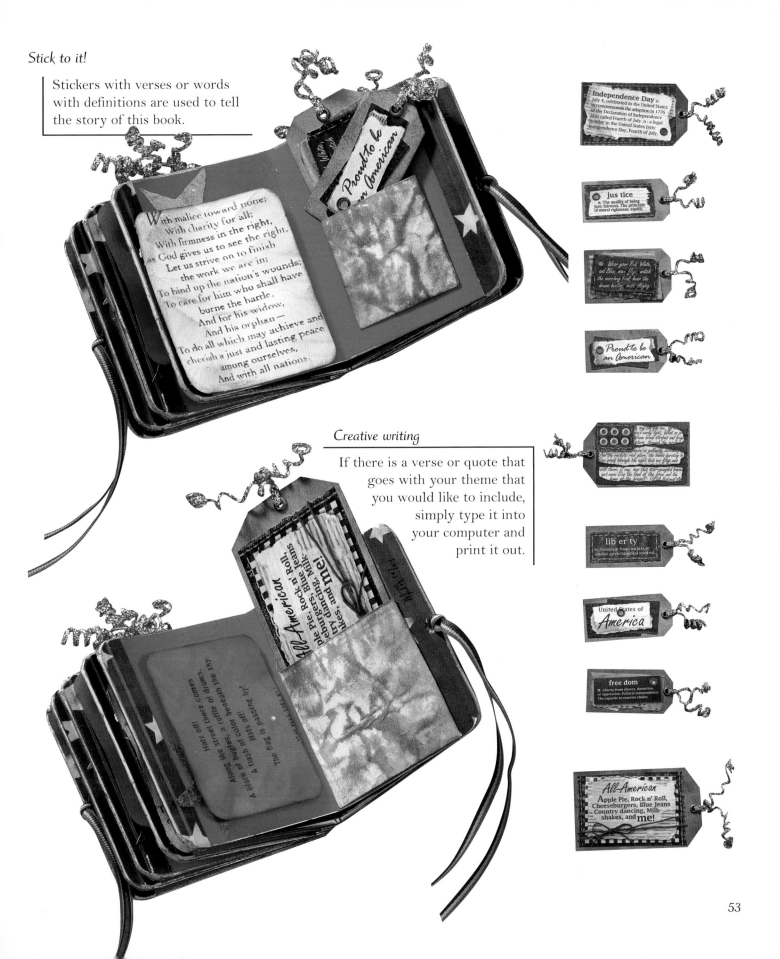

Stick to it!

Stickers with verses or words with definitions are used to tell the story of this book.

Independence Day n. July 4, celebrated in the United States to commemorate the adoption in 1776 of the Declaration of Independence. Also called Fourth of July. n : a legal holiday in the United States [syn: Independence Day, Fourth of July,

jus tice n. The quality of being just; fairness. The principle of moral rightness; equity.

Wear your Red, White, and Blue; wave flags; watch the marching band; hear the drums beating; rise; singing

Proud to be an American

lib er ty n. freedom from unjust or undue governmental control.

United States of America

free dom n. Liberty from slavery, detention, or oppression. Political independence. The capacity to exercise choice.

All-American Apple Pie, Rock n' Roll, Cheeseburgers, Blue Jeans Country dancing, Milk-shakes, and me!

With malice toward none;
With charity for all;
With firmness in the right,
As God gives us to see the right,
Let us strive on to finish
the work we are in;
To bind up the nation's wounds;
To care for him who shall have
borne the battle,
And for his widow,
And his orphan —
To do all which may achieve and
cherish a just and lasting peace
among ourselves,
And with all nations.

Creative writing

If there is a verse or quote that goes with your theme that you would like to include, simply type it into your computer and print it out.

All-American Apple Pie, Rock n' Jeans pie, Blue Jeans, Milk-eburgers, try dancing, and **me!** akes, and me!

Hats off!
Along the street there comes
A blare of bugles, a ruffle of drums,
A flash of color beneath the sky:
Hats off!
The flag is passing by!

8
project

What you need to get started:

Materials
- Old book

Adhesives
- Liquid adhesive
- Paper adhesive

Ephemera
- Alphabet letter stickers
- Assorted embellishments
- Cards
- Fibers
- Memorabilia
- Photos

Paints
- Metallic acrylic paints: cranberry; raisin

Papers
- Decorative Papers

Tools & Other Supplies
- Craft knife
- Distress ink pads
- Rubber stamps with love-related images or verses

How do I work with an old book?

Using older books gives you the opportunity to glue sections together to cut niches, or make doors or windows, for displaying memorabilia or special trinkets and photos.

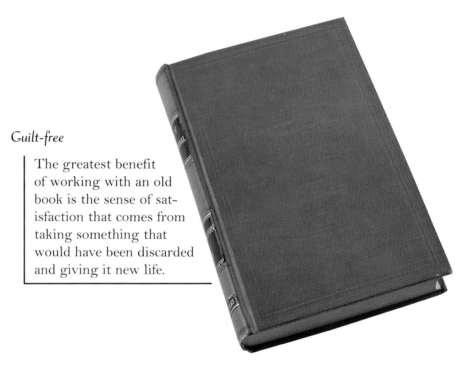

Guilt-free

The greatest benefit of working with an old book is the sense of satisfaction that comes from taking something that would have been discarded and giving it new life.

Love Notes

Here's how:

1. Refer to **How do I prepare the covers?** on pages 19–20. Prepare the front and back covers.

2. Divide book into sections. Determine the pages needed for a niche. Refer to **How do I glue a block of pages together?** on pages 21–22. Glue the block of pages together.

3. Refer to **How do I cut niches, windows, or doors?** on pages 26–28. Cut a niche into the block of pages.

Finding your niche

A niche is used as a place for attaching cherished photos or dimensional elements that you want to give special attention or make stand out on the page.

4. Refer to **How do I fold or tear pages to create pockets?** on page 23–24. Fold a section to form layered vertical pockets.

5. Refer to **How do I add pockets for tags?** on pages 25–26. Form pockets for tags.

6. Refer to **How do I add paint to the pages or covers?** on pages 28–29. Paint covers.

7. Paint sections inside the book.

8. Refer to **How do I collage?** on pages 30–31. Collage decorative papers onto front cover.

9. Add a photo and embellish niche as desired.

10. Make tags for pockets.

11. Refer to **How can I use rubber stamps and ink pads?** on pages 29–30. Stamp images or verses onto inside pages.

12. Adhere cards, letters, memorabilia, photos, etc., to inside pages.

13. Tie fibers along spine of book.

14. Embellish cover with ephemera as desired.

Layered vertical pockets
add dimension and create
a place for including a
few coordinating tags.

*It is
through
the miracle
of love
that
we discover
the fullness
of life*

FOR THE
One I Love

Year by year,
our love unfolds,
each moment
more beautiful
than the last.

Flowery language

Both vintage and
contemporary cards
and postcards are
wonderful sources
for floral motifs and
inspirational verse.

57

9
project

What you need to get started:

Materials
- Dictionary

Adhesives
- Foam glue
- Liquid adhesive
- Sepia decoupage glue
- Sheet of double-sided tape

Ephemera
- Assorted embellishments
- Old belt or leather strap with buckle
- Game tiles

Paints
- Acrylic paints: slate blue; brown

Tools & Other Supplies
- Archival ink pads
- Craft knife
- Foam-core board
- Rubber stamp

How can I use only the cover of an old book?

Removing the pages from a book and replacing them with a box made from foam-core board gives you an ideal place to keep special treasures or letters and cards.

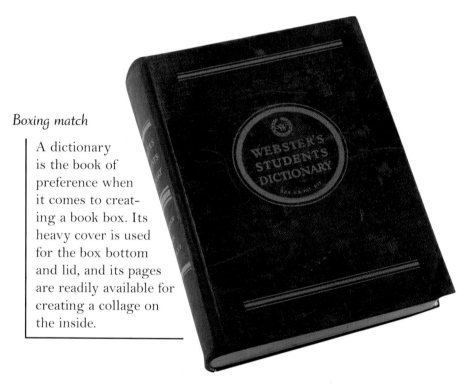

Boxing match

A dictionary is the book of preference when it comes to creating a book box. Its heavy cover is used for the box bottom and lid, and its pages are readily available for creating a collage on the inside.

Outside the Box

Here's how:

1. Refer to **How do I prepare the covers?** on pages 19–20. Prepare front and back covers.

2. Refer to **How do I remove pages from inside the book?** on page 20. Remove the pages from the book by cutting along the spine with the craft knife.

3. Measure the height, width, and depth of the pages removed.

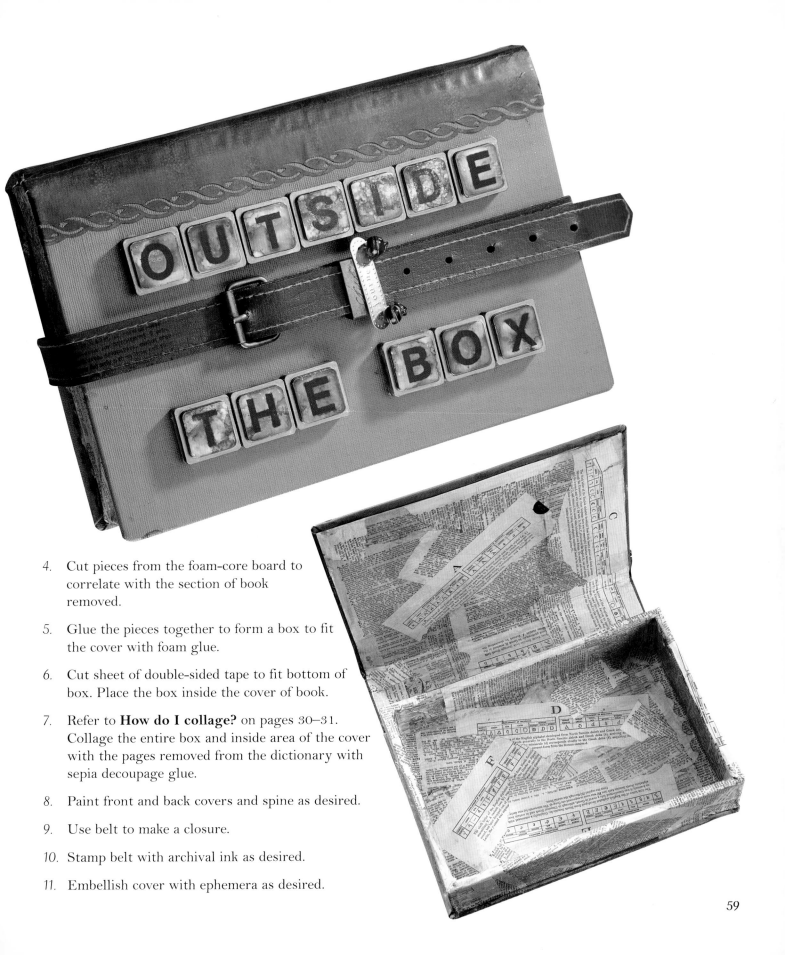

4. Cut pieces from the foam-core board to correlate with the section of book removed.

5. Glue the pieces together to form a box to fit the cover with foam glue.

6. Cut sheet of double-sided tape to fit bottom of box. Place the box inside the cover of book.

7. Refer to **How do I collage?** on pages 30–31. Collage the entire box and inside area of the cover with the pages removed from the dictionary with sepia decoupage glue.

8. Paint front and back covers and spine as desired.

9. Use belt to make a closure.

10. Stamp belt with archival ink as desired.

11. Embellish cover with ephemera as desired.

10 project

What you need to get started:

Materials

- Shaped book

Adhesives

- Decoupage glue
- Paper adhesive
- Spray adhesive

Ephemera

- Assorted embellishments
- Buckle
- Computer-generated poems and verses
- Felt strip
- Handkerchief
- Necklace chain
- Photos

Paints

- Violet light body pearlescent paint

Papers

- Decorative papers
- Envelope

Tools & Other Supplies

- 18-gauge gold wire
- Distress inks
- Metallic pen
- Rubber stamps
- Sponge

How do I turn a shaped board book into a gift?

Look beyond the subject matter of books. The shape alone can suggest a theme: a pumpkin becomes a ladies purse (mother/grandmother), a triangle shape can represent a Christmas tree (holiday), and a book with a handle can become a suitcase (travel/trip).

Shape shifting

Board books are available in many different shapes and sizes. You can use both these characteristics to the advantage of the altered art theme you have selected.

And now it's your turn
To have a treat, too,
Just like your pals, Piglet
And Winnie the Pooh.

This isn't candy
Or something to eat.
Just lift up this flap
For a Halloween treat . . . .

Classy Lady

Here's how:

1. Refer to **How do I prepare the covers?** on pages 19–20. Prepare front and back covers.

2. Refer to **How do I glue pages together?** on pages 20–21. Glue pages together as desired.

3. Refer to **How do I cut niches, windows, or doors?** on pages 26–28. Form a door and a niche in the glued pages.

4. Cut papers to fit pages. Spray adhesive onto backs of the papers, then apply to pages.

5. Refer to **How can I use rubber stamps and ink pads?** on pages 29–30. Age paper edges with inks.

6. Refer to **How do I collage?** on pages 30–31. Collage the cover with decorative papers.

7. Glue an envelope onto one page to hold a handkerchief.

8. Add a photo or computer-generated verse into the window. Add poems or messages or other related ephemera into recessed opening.

9. Embellish the cover with ephemera as desired.

10. Attach a closure made from the felt strip with a buckle attached.

11. Attach an old necklace chain with wire to create a purse handle.

Beautiful friend

A round mirror is ringed with a strand of pearls and outlined with alphabet stickers that spell out how this friend is seen by others.

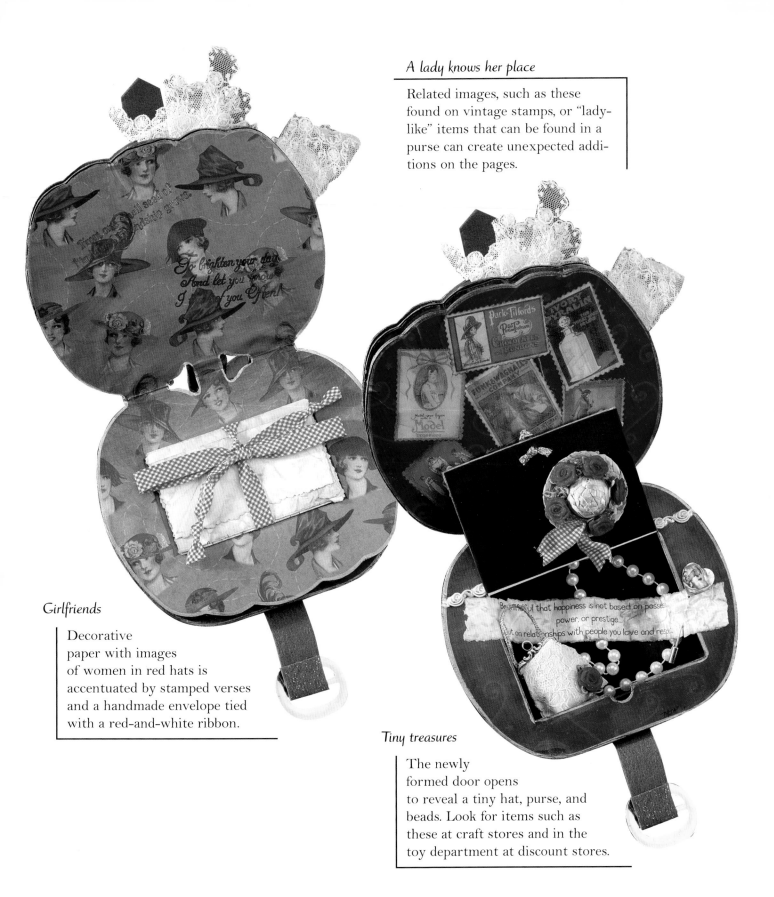

Related images, such as these found on vintage stamps, or "lady-like" items that can be found in a purse can create unexpected additions on the pages.

Girlfriends

Decorative paper with images of women in red hats is accentuated by stamped verses and a handmade envelope tied with a red-and-white ribbon.

Tiny treasures

The newly formed door opens to reveal a tiny hat, purse, and beads. Look for items such as these at craft stores and in the toy department at discount stores.

11
project

What you need to get started:

Materials
- Book of choice

Adhesives
- Paper adhesive
- Liquid adhesive

Ephemera
- Assorted embellishments
- Fibers
- Ribbons
- Tags

Paints
- Dimensional paints: various colors

Papers
- Decorative papers
- Cardstock

Tools & Other Supplies
- Cosmetic sponge
- Distress ink pads
- Flat brush
- Lace border punch
- Rubber stamps
- Slot paper punch

How do I use an old book for a "round robin" with a group of friends?

Usually in a "round robin" the book will travel from friend to friend. Each chooses a section of the book and alters it as desired. This book was divided into sections and tagged for each friend.

New deal

Although this book—altered to contain pocket pages and act as a carrier for altered art tags—was found at a thrift store, it was selected because it was fairly new with relatively clean, white pages that would be left largely undecorated.

Girls Just Want to Have Fun

Here's how:

1. Refer to **How do I prepare the covers?** on pages 19–20. Prepare front and back covers.

2. Refer to **How do I remove pages from inside the book?** on page 20. Divide book into sections. Remove some pages if necessary.

3. Refer to **How do I fold or tear pages to create pockets?** on page 23–24. Fold pages to form diagonal pockets—one per person participating.

4. Cut and punch decorative papers to trim edges of pockets.

5. Refer to **How do I add paint to the pages or covers?** on pages 28–29. Paint pages in desired colors by sponging, brushing, or using other desired technique.

6. Using rubber stamps, add names, images, or more to pages.

7. Paint and embellish cover as desired. Tie on fibers.

8. Send the book to friends with blank tags and extra papers. They will decorate the tags and pages according to the chosen theme.

Go girl!

Pocket pages are tabbed
with mini tags with the
names of friends involved
in the "round robin." The
artists develop their own
concept of what it means
to be a girl—all on a
paper tag.

12
project

What you need to get started:

Materials
- Children's musical book

Adhesive
- Decoupage glue
- Iron-on fabric adhesive
- Liquid adhesive
- Paper adhesive

Ephemera
- Alphabet letters
- Brads
- Buttons
- Clipart
- Fibers
- Lace
- Photos
- Ribbons
- Stickers
- Vintage baby images

Papers
- Decorative papers
- Envelopes

Tools & Other Supplies
- Craft iron
- Fabric

How do I use a children's musical book to create a baby keepsake?

Books that play music add an element of fun to making a keepsake book. This book played the tune Twinkle, Twinkle Little Star. The words to the song were computer generated to fit the panel from where the music comes. The specific area to play the song is embellished with stars.

Music maker

The built-in music player provides an inspiring starting place for selecting a theme for this altered-art book.

Baby Gift

Here's how:

1. Refer to **How do I prepare the covers?** on pages 19–20. Prepare front and back covers.

2. Refer to **How do I glue pages together?** on pages 20–21. Determine pages to be glued together; glue accordingly.

New arrival

Vintage images of babies are combined with gingham and striped decorative papers to create a delicate setting for the newborn's picture—hidden here behind a window—and birth announcement information.

3. Following manufacturer's directions, prepare fabric with iron-on adhesive.

4. Cut fabric into strips. Weave strips to make an interlocking piece. Using craft iron, adhere the piece onto the cover of the book.

5. Refer to **How do I collage?** on pages 30–31. Collage decorative papers to the back cover with liquid adhesive. Adhere paper items or images onto front in the same manner. Allow to dry.

6. Refer to **How do I fold or tear pages to create pockets?** on page 23–24. Fold over first and last pages for pockets.

7. Collage decorative papers onto pockets and other pages with decoupage glue. Adhere clipart or computer-generated words onto pages. Allow to dry.

8. Refer to **How do I cut niches, windows, or doors?** on pages 26–28. Choose a page on which to cut a window or windows for photos.

9. Place photos on the following page to correspond with the windows.

10. Embellish cover and pages as desired with buttons, stickers, and other ephemera.

Traditional nursery rhymes and verses decorate these pages. CD envelopes make perfect frames for precious baby photos on the pages below.

OUR BOOK

PRECIOUS (presh´-es) 1. of great worth 2. beloved; cherished

MIRACLE (mir´-e-kel) 1. an event or action unexplained by scientific law 2. an awesome or unimaginable outcome

BEAUTIFUL (byoot´-e-ful) 1. pleasingly attractive physical appearance 2. lovely; fine to behold 3. delicate and favorable

BABY! MY BABY

You're such a sweet wonder, and daily surprise; With glimpses of heaven, I catch from your eyes. Through beautiful blue, that you brought from the skies. Baby! My baby!

Oh, how could you bring so much joy from above? For you are so tiny to bring so much love. The angels will miss it, and miss you, my dove. Baby! My baby!

Why is it you're happy when in my embrace? And why is the wonder that shines in your face? Is my love like God's? Does it make every place Heaven? My baby!

CHERUB (cher´-eb) 1. a type of angel characterized as a chubby, rosy cheeked child with wings 2. a child with a sweet, innocent face

WYNKEN, BLYNKEN, AND NOD
EUGENE FIELD

God made the world with its towering trees, majestic mountains and restless seas. Then paused and said, "It needs one more thing, someone to laugh and dance and sing. To walk in the woods and gather flowers."

So God made little girls, with laughing eyes and bouncing curls. With joyful hearts and infectious smiles, enchanting ways and feminine wiles. And when he completed the task He'd begun, he was pleased and proud of the job He'd done. For the world, when seen through a little girl's eyes, greatly resembles Paradise.

sweet dreams

CURLY LOCKS

One, two, three, four, five, Once I caught a fish alive, Six, seven, eight, nine, ten, But I let him go again. Why did you let him go? Because he bit my finger so. Which finger did he bite? This little one upon the right.

TEN FINGERS

Curly locks! curly locks! wilt thou be mine? Thou shalt not wash dishes, nor yet feed the swine: But sit on a cushion, and sew a fine seam, And feed upon strawberries, sugar, and cream!

Twinkle, twinkle, little star, How I wonder what you are, Up above the world so high, Like a diamond in the sky.

When the blazing sun is gone, When he nothing shines upon, Then you show your little light, Twinkle, twinkle, all the night.

Then the traveler in the dark, Thanks you for your tiny spark, How could he see where to go, If you did not twinkle so.

In the dark blue sky you keep, Often through my curtains peep, For you never shut your eye, Till the sun is in the sky.

As your bright and tiny spark, Lights the traveler in the dark, Though I know not what you are, Twinkle, twinkle, little star.

Twinkle, twinkle, little star, How I wonder what you are, Up above the world so high, Like a diamond in the sky.

When the blazing sun is gone, When he nothing shines upon, Then you show your little light, Twinkle, twinkle, all the night.

Then the traveler in the dark, Thanks you for your tiny spark, How could he see where to go, If you did not twinkle on.

In the dark blue sky you keep, Often through my curtains peep, For you never shut your eye, Till the sun is in the sky.

As your bright and tiny spark, Lights the traveler in the dark, Though I know not what you are, Twinkle, twinkle, little star.

I ♥ YOU

ART washes away from the Soul the dust of everyday life.

Vision

A VERY HAPPY BIRTHDAY
To greet you now this merry day
This little Card I send,
And ever pray that gladness may
Your path in life attend.

discover

Art is an Adventure that never seems to end.
—Jason
Los Cerros Middle School

Art is your personal diary where you may **color** your thoughts and emotions on a **page.**
—Sara—
Los Cerros Middle School

Section 3: Projects Beyond the Basics

1

project

Use a board book as a story frame

Honor Him

What you need to get started:

Materials
- Board book

Adhesives
- Liquid adhesive

Ephemera
- Buttons
- Eyelets
- Fibers
- Metal alphabet letters and numbers
- Photo

Paints
- Metallic acrylic paints: denim; raisin

Papers
- Decorative paper

Tools & Other Supplies
- Craft knife
- Eyelet-setting tools
- Ruler

Here's how:

1. Refer to **How do I prepare the covers?** on pages 19–20. Prepare front and back covers.

2. Mark an opening on desired pages for the photo.

3. Using craft knife, cut along lines.

4. Refer to **How do I add paint to the pages or covers?** on pages 28–29. Sponge the pages with acrylic paints.

5. Adhere decorative papers onto front and back covers.

6. Refer to **How do I glue a block of pages together?** on pages 21–22. Glue the painted pages together.

7. Adhere desired embellishments and photo.

2
project

What you need to get started:

Materials
- Small, old book

Adhesives
- Liquid adhesive

Ephemera
- Buttons
- Clipart or stickers with verses
- Fibers
- Small puzzle

Papers
- Decorative papers
- Gold tissue paper

Tools & Other Supplies
- Craft knife

Make a tiny treasure book

Hidden Message

Here's how:

1. Refer to **How do I prepare the covers?** on pages 19–20. Prepare front and back covers.

2. Refer to **How do I cut niches, windows, or doors?** on pages 26–28. Use all pages to create a niche, with the exception of the first three or four—these pages can be glued together.

3. Glue niche to back cover. Allow to dry.

4. Cover the niche with tissue paper.

5. Refer to **How do I collage?** on pages 30–31. Collage front and back covers with decorative papers.

6. Adhere stickers or clipart onto puzzle to create a message.

7. Using craft knife, cut along the puzzle lines. Place puzzle pieces into niche.

8. Embellish cover with ephemera as desired.

Inside out

A small niche like this one can hold other objects, such as a lock of hair, a pressed flower, or special piece of jewelry. Let the object determine how you will decorate the cover.

Puzzling pictures

Blank white puzzles can be found in craft stores and also can be altered by covering them with photos or papers and adhering small tokens or charms.

3

project

What you need to get started:

Materials

- Dollar-store spiral scrapbooks (2)

Adhesives

- Decoupage glue
- Fabric adhesive
- Sheet of double-sided tape

Ephemera

- Decorative tag
- Memorabilia
- Metal word strip
- Photos
- Ribbons

Papers

- Decorative papers

Tools & Other Supplies

- Border punches
- Craft scissors
- Distress ink pads
- Fabrics
- Rubber stamps
- Tiny rickrack
- Utility knife

Alter a scrapbook album

Happy Holidays

Here's how:

1. Refer to **How do I prepare the covers?** on pages 19–20. Prepare front and back covers.

2. Divide the front covers of each book equally and mark for cutting. Using utility knife, cut at markings.

3. Adhere fabric or decorative papers onto each back cover.

4. Using border punches, create a decorative edge on each inside page.

5. Cut sheet of double-sided tape to fit the size of the back cover. With spines opposite each other, overlap the back covers with the double-sided tape sandwiched between the two.

6. Cut coordinating fabric and paper pieces; adhere them onto the front covers with decoupage glue. Adhere rickrack with fabric adhesive.

7. Refer to **How can I use rubber stamps and ink pads?** on pages 29–30. Punch edges of inside pages with border punch. Distress edges with inks as desired. Collate the pages from each book.

8 . Stamp images or words onto pages; add photos or other related memorabilia.

9. Embellish front cover with decorative tag.

10. Tie ribbons to the spiral edges of scrapbooks, then trim.

11. If desired, center and punch a hole on the outer edges of both covers, then add ribbon for a tie closure.

All decked out

The top cover is decorated with coordinating squares of fabric, which are accentuated with ivory rickrack. When the cut flaps of the top covers are open, you can see how the blank scrapbook pages have been edged and collated—ready for placement of favorite memorabilia.

4
project

What you need to get started:

Materials
- Papier-mâché book box

Adhesives
- Decoupage glue
- Fabric adhesive
- Thick white adhesive

Ephemera
- Assorted embellishments
- Postcards
- Trims

Papers
- Decorative papers

Tools & Other Supplies
- Craft scissors
- Gold leafing sheets and adhesive
- Leather or fabric piece for spine

Use a premade book-shaped papier-mâché box

Stationery Holder

Here's how:

1. Cut paper to fit inside cover and inside bottom of box, then adhere in place with decoupage glue.

2. Adhere desired papers onto outside of box with decoupage glue.

3. Adhere leather onto book spine with fabric adhesive.

4. Following manufacturer's directions, adhere gold leafing to "page" section on outside of box.

5. Embellish box cover as desired.

6. Embellish postcards as desired.

7. Place postcards inside box.

Mail time

Vintage images are stamped with tender verses, then layered on two to three different colors of cardstock, creating personalized postcards that can be tied together or placed loose in the box.

5

project

What you need to get started:

Materials

Adhesives
- Quick-dry adhesive

Ephemera
- Alphabet letter stickers
- Bottle caps
- Brads
- Clippings
- Creative clips
- Eyelets
- Mesh
- Ribbons
- Slide mounts
- Stickers
- Verses

Paints
- Metallic acrylic paints: gold; verdigris

Papers
- Large tags

Tools & Other Supplies
- ¼"-thick balsa wood
- Cutting tool
- Distress ink pads
- Eyelet-setting tools
- Rubber stamps
- Ruler
- Split-locking ring

Make a tag book

Dream, Imagine, Create

Here's how:

1. Trace tag shape onto wood two times.

2. Using cutting tool and ruler, cut out shapes.

3. Using a piercing tool, carefully bore a hole into wooden tags.

4. Paint wooden tags with gold acrylic to create book covers.

5. Refer to **How can I use rubber stamps and ink pads?** on pages 29–30. Distress paper tags with inks.

6. Add stickers, photos, and verses to paper tags with brads, clips, and eyelets.

7. Embellish wooden tags with verdigris acrylic, clippings, slide mounts, and bottle caps as desired.

8. Place all paper and wooden tags on ring. Close.

9. Tie pieces of ribbon onto ring.

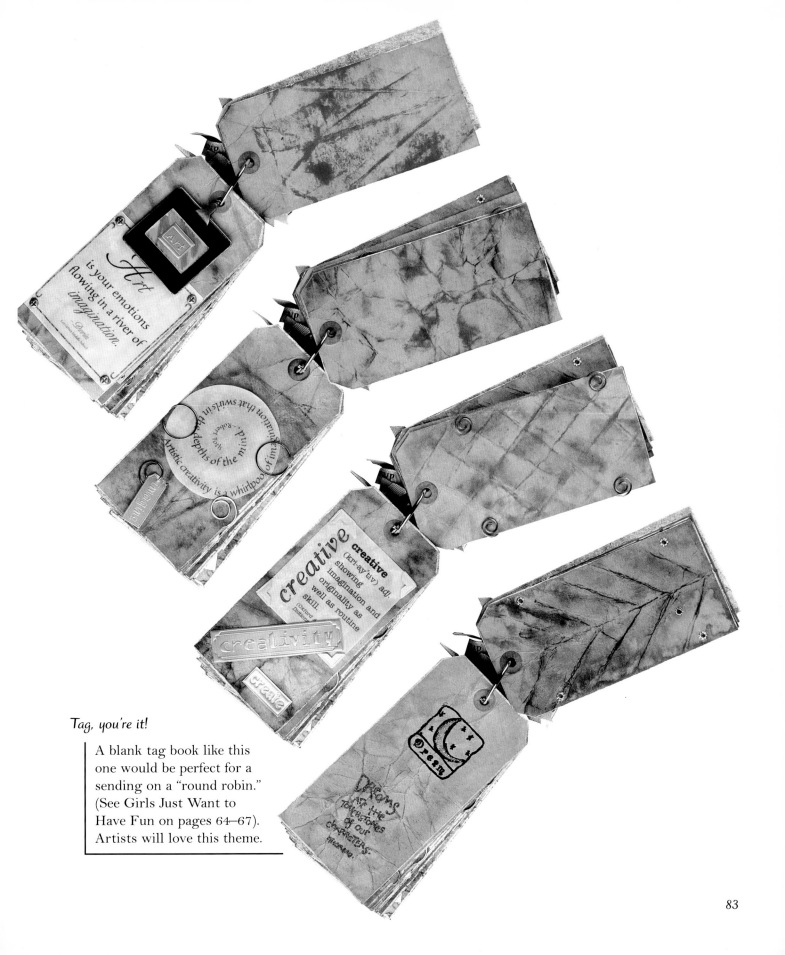

Art *is your emotions flowing in a river of imagination.* —Death

Artistic creativity is a whirlpool of imagination that swirls in the depths of the mind. —Robert

creative
creative (krī-ay´tiv) adj.
showing
imagination and
originality as
well as routine
skill.
(Oxford
Dictionary)

creativity

create

Dreams are the touchstones of our characters. —Thoreau

Tag, you're it!

A blank tag book like this one would be perfect for a sending on a "round robin." (See Girls Just Want to Have Fun on pages 64–67). Artists will love this theme.

6
project

What you need to get started:

Materials
- Used cassette holder or similarly sized box

Adhesives
- Decoupage glue

Ephemera
- Assorted embellishments
- Book-related clipart

Paints
- Metallic acrylic paints: bottle; pesto; terra-cotta

Papers
- Paper or fabric for lining

Tools & Other Supplies
- Sponge

Decorate a books-on-tape box

Books on Tape

Here's how:

1. Refer to **How do I add paint to the pages or covers?** on pages 28–29. Sponge paints onto the outside of the box. Allow to dry.

2. Adhere paper onto the inside of the box with decoupage glue. Allow to dry.

3. Embellish top of box as desired with book-related clipart.

Dress up a photo journal

Travel Memories

Here's how:

1. Remove the cardboard inserts from photo holders. Cut new inserts from cardstock or reuse the existing inserts.

2. Refer to **How do I collage?** on pages 30–31. Collage with decorative papers.

3. Cut adhesive sheet to fit the covers of holders.

4. Apply one sheet between each holder.

5. Cut fibers three times the height of the book. Cut lengths for each holder.

6. Place the fibers into center of each holder.

7. Tie fibers to form a knot at the top of the holders or along the spine of the book.

8. Embellish as desired.

7
project

What you need to get started:

Materials
- Plastic photo holders (3)

Adhesives
- Sheet of double-sided tape

Ephemera
- Assorted embellishments
- Fibers

Papers
- Cardstock
- Decorative papers

Tools & Other Supplies
- Craft scissors

What you need to get started:

Materials
- Large playing cards

Adhesives
- Antique decoupage glue
- Double-sided tape: ⅛"; ¼"

Ephemera
- Alphabet buttons
- Brads
- Eyelets
- Photos
- Ribbon
- Thin jute cord

Papers
- Decorative papers

Tools & Other Supplies
- Craft scissors
- Distress ink pads
- Eyelet-setting tools
- Metal foil tape
- Sticker maker

Make a book out of playing cards

In the Cards

Here's how:

Note: Each page will require a set of two cards.

1. Refer to **How do I collage?** on pages 30–31. Collage decorative papers onto one side of each card.

2. Tear edges around photos.

3. Refer to **How can I use rubber stamps and ink pads?** on pages 29–30. Apply inks onto edges of photos.

4. Using sticker maker, apply adhesive onto photos. Adhere photos onto front of cards.

5. Adhere double-sided tape along the edges of one of the cards in each set. Remove tape backing. Place the remaining card in the set on top, aligning the edges. Repeat procedure for each set of cards.

6. Fold metal foil tape around all edges of each combined set of cards.

7. Place eyelets along both long edges of each set of cards.

8. Arrange cards in a row as desired. Join sets of cards together by threading jute cord through eyelets of two consecutive cards and knot ends. Keep length between cards short, but long enough to fold cards accordion style. Repeat for each set of eyelets.

9. Cut a length of ribbon and attach to the front card with paper brads. Tie ribbon into a bow.

10. Fold cards accordion style.

11. Embellish book front with alphabet buttons as desired.

9
project

What you need to get started:

Materials
- Empty gum or mint tin

Adhesives
- Liquid adhesive

Ephemera
- Assorted embellishments
- Chain or handmade necklace
- Clipart

Paints
- Bronze light body metallic acrylic paint

Papers
- Heavy-weight paper
- Lightweight cardstocks

Tools & Other Supplies
- 20-gauge wire
- Metal punch tool
- Small foam-core-board piece

Use a gum or mint tin

Gum Tin Pendant

Here's how:

1. Trace the shape of the tin onto heavy-weight paper, creating a pattern.

2. Use traced shape as a pattern to cut one piece of foam-core board.

3. Accordion-fold one sheet of lightweight cardstock the width of the pattern. Trace pattern and cut out.

4. Paint outside of tin.

5. Punch two small holes into top of tin.

6. Insert a small piece of wire to form a loop. Cut excess wire and bend wire end to back of tin.

7. Glue foam-core board onto inside of tin.

8. Write a message or adhere clipart onto folded paper.

9. Glue onto foam-core board inside tin.

10. Add a chain onto wire loop.

11. Embellish outside of tin as desired. *Note: For this piece, a figure was fashioned using a variety of ephemera such as a watch face, metal tags, brads, tiny pins, spools, buttons, fibers, and a clay face.*

10 project

What you need to get started:

Materials
- Small matchbox

Adhesives
- Double-sided ¼" tape

Ephemera
- Buttons
- Chain
- Charms
- Cord
- Pin clasp
- Watch face

Papers
- Decorative papers
- Plain text-weight paper

Tools & Other Supplies
- Craft scissors
- Cosmetic sponge
- Distress inks: black, mustard
- Rubber stamps with related verses

Use a matchbox to make a pin or pendant

Matchbox Pendant

Here's how:

1. Remove inner box from matchbox sleeve.

2. Cut decorative paper to fit outside matchbox sleeve.

3. Apply double-sided tape onto paper. Tape paper piece around sleeve.

4. Cut and accordion-fold text-weight paper to fit inside box.

5. Stamp verses onto folded paper. Age edges with mustard ink.

6. Glue folded paper into box.

7. Slide inner box into box sleeve.

8. Glue a pin clasp onto sleeve back.

9. Embellish sleeve front and sides as desired.

Ticktock box

The message hidden inside this tiny box, stamped in black ink and aged at the edges with mustard ink, furthers the antique feeling of the vintage watch face and charms displayed on the outside.

Women are like buttons, they hold things together.

The time to be happy is now... the place to be happy is here...

Every day of your life is a page of your history

Make an envelope book

What you need to get started:

Materials

• Kraft mailing envelopes (6)

Adhesives

• Iron-on fabric adhesive

• Fabric glue

Ephemera

• Lace

• Ribbon

Papers

• Decorative paper

• Heavy-weight cardboard

Tools & Other Supplies

• Craft iron

• Craft scissors

• Decorative-edged scissors

• Embossing ink and powder

• Fabric

• Heat tool

• Paper trimmer

• Rubber stamp

Garden Seed Saver

Here's how:

1. Using a paper trimmer, cut approximately ¼" of the closed end from each envelope.

2. Fold envelopes in half.

3. Turn sealing flaps to outside.

4. Stack the envelopes, alternating front and back, facing up. Glue the abutting flaps together. Continue for all envelopes.

5. Cut two cardboard pieces ½" larger than folded envelopes on all sides.

6. Cut decorative paper ½" larger on all sides than cardboard pieces. Glue decorative paper onto one side of each cardboard piece, folding and gluing paper edges to opposite side of cardboard.

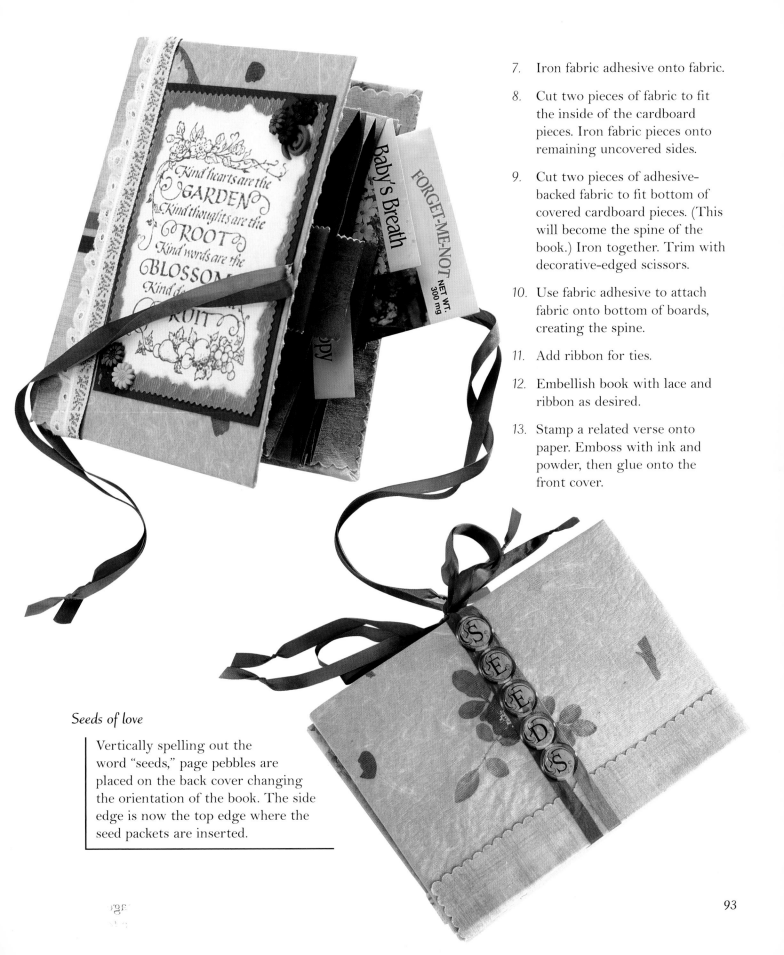

7. Iron fabric adhesive onto fabric.

8. Cut two pieces of fabric to fit the inside of the cardboard pieces. Iron fabric pieces onto remaining uncovered sides.

9. Cut two pieces of adhesive-backed fabric to fit bottom of covered cardboard pieces. (This will become the spine of the book.) Iron together. Trim with decorative-edged scissors.

10. Use fabric adhesive to attach fabric onto bottom of boards, creating the spine.

11. Add ribbon for ties.

12. Embellish book with lace and ribbon as desired.

13. Stamp a related verse onto paper. Emboss with ink and powder, then glue onto the front cover.

Seeds of love

Vertically spelling out the word "seeds," page pebbles are placed on the back cover changing the orientation of the book. The side edge is now the top edge where the seed packets are inserted.

What you need to get started:

Materials
- Old book

Adhesives
- Paper adhesive
- Thick white adhesive

Ephemera
- Clay face
- Feathers for wings
- Fibers
- Foam alphabet stickers
- Old cotton lace
- Stickers with fairy theme
- Tags

Paints
- Metallic acrylic paints

Tools & Other Supplies
- Brads or 24-gauge wire
- Gold leafing pen
- Rubber stamp with doll figure

Make a book for holding tags

Garden Fairies

Here's how:

1. Refer to **How do I remove pages from inside the book?** on page 20. Divide book into sections. Use about 10 pages for each, more if the pages are thin. Remove pages from the back of the book if necessary.

2. Refer to **How do I add pockets for tags?** on pages 25–26. Between each section, add a pocket for a tag.

3. Hold the sections together with brads or wire.

4. Refer to **How do I add paint to the pages or covers?** on pages 28–29. Stipple the pages and tags with thinned acrylic paints to add color. Allow to dry.

5. Add the themed stickers onto the painted pages.

6. Use any remaining stickers on tags. Place tags into hidden pockets.

7. Sponge the front and back covers with acrylic paints.

8. Change the color of the foam stickers with the gold leafing pen. Allow to dry.

9. Construct a fairy from stamped image—use old lace for the dress, clay for the face, and feathers for the wings.

10. Adhere fairy onto front cover with thick white adhesive. Allow to dry.

11. Adhere foam stickers onto front cover.

In the garden

Leaving text blocks so they can be viewed on the pages adds to the design of the book. Tags are painted and embellished to coordinate with the look of the pages that hold them.

Section 4: Gallery

Belt

A worn belt takes on a new life after it is painted and adorned with papers and small flat ephemera.

From plain to pizazz

A new belt also can be altered according to a theme, creating a unique accessory that adds something special to an ordinary outfit.

Suitcase

A very old discarded suitcase is used as a holder for scrapbooks from trips. It is covered with brown kraft paper or torn pieces from old grocery bags. The paper is applied with an antique decoupage finish. Travel stickers are added. An old luggage tag is painted and attached to the handle. The handle is wrapped in torn pieces of muslin to cover the torn, dirty handle. Old belts are glued on to add an old-fashioned look.

Saving scraps

Many scrapbook albums have inside pages that also can be embellished in the altered art style and accented with photos from a particular occasion.

Memory Scrapbooks

Spiral albums are decorated with mementos, photos, and other memorabilia from trips. The Suitcase on page 98 makes the perfect container to hold the albums. It is large enough to hold about four similarly sized albums.

Denim Vest

An old worn vest gets an altered look by adding other flea-market finds such as an old lace collar, checkered bias tape, baby rickrack, and a handkerchief. Some buttons are added and a zipper pull made from bottle caps gives the vest a unique touch. Stamped images are added here and there just for fun.

Monogram Bag

Found at a thrift store, this purse was layered with various papers. Then letters from and old anagram game were used for the monogram.

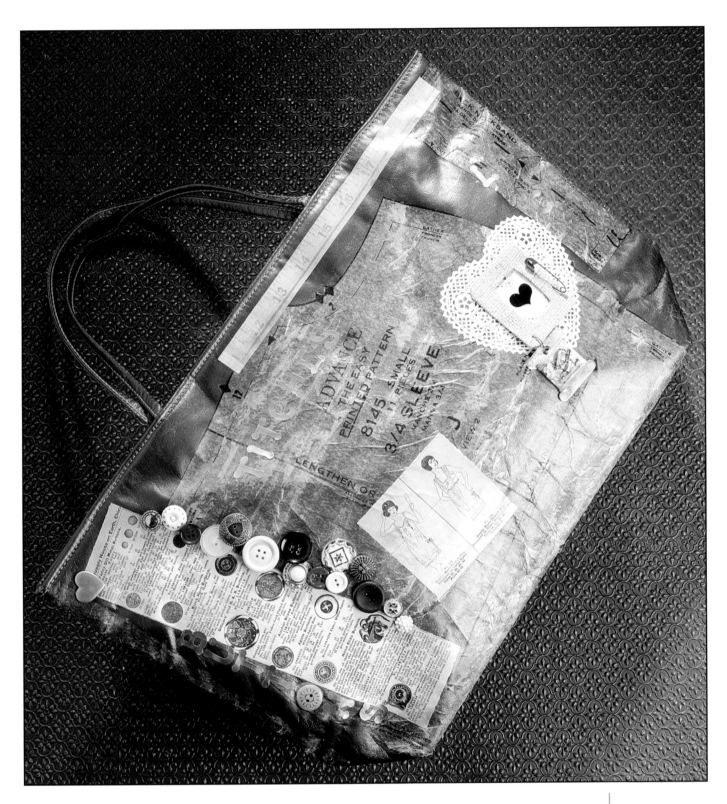

Needlework Bag

Another thrift store treasure. It is collaged with pieces from an old sewing pattern. It is also embellished with stickers, doilies, buttons, and needlecraft items.

Gloves

A plain pair of leather gloves has some old lace from a collar sewn onto the edges. A variety of old buttons are also sewn on to finish the edge. A heart-shaped brad is glued onto the ring finger.

Collage Tray

This tray is made from an unfinished frame and decorative cabinet handles. It shows off a variety of pressed leaves and flowers. It is embellished with stickers, buttons, and metal words.

Family Memories

An inexpensive album is collaged with torn handmade papers and clippings, then embellished with old photos, game tiles, and glitter glue. The finished album can be used to capture memories of celebrating a special day such as an anniversary.

Fabric & Lace

This papier-mâché box is covered with paper, fabric, and old lace. A glass drawer pull is added for a handle. Wooden feet are glued to the bottom and adorned with glass beads. This piece can be used as a purse or jewelry box.

My "Illinois" Purse

Made from a wooden cigar box, this purse is covered with maps, music sheets, old postcards, and a jeans pocket, to represent my home state. It features my favorite colors—red, white, and blue.

Evening Bag

This is another version of a cigar box purse with a more elegant look. The box is covered with reprints of pages from an old Sears catalog showing purses. It is trimmed with old-fashioned black braid and a large antique button for a closure.

Adventure Tag Necklace

Tiny paper tags are collaged with bits of decorative paper, then embellished with clipped words of inspiration and paper pebbles that spell out "adventure." The tags are combined with glass beads in the same color scheme on a wire necklace.

Sweet Land of Liberty Deco

"Deco" is the name we give an altered book that is created in a "round robin." Seven to eight people usually work on the book. The originator begins with a theme, then that person forms a book, making the front and back cover and the first page. A list of participants is included and the deco travels from person to person. Each person adds a page, interpreting the theme in his or her own way. It is returned to the original artist. The theme of this deco is "Sweet Land of Liberty." Participants used various images of the Statue of Liberty and the flag of the United States.

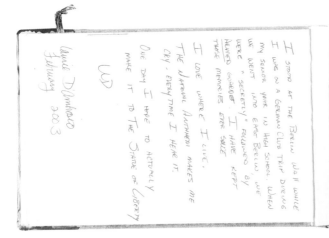

Home Sweet Home Deco

The theme selected for this deco is "Home Sweet Home." The book was constructed from book board, fabrics, and heavy cardstock pages. The artists who worked on this little book designed their pages around a favorite poem or verse about home. They added photos, clipart, and decorative papers to match.

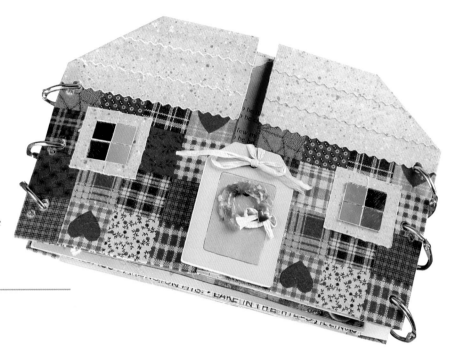

Little flipper

The originator of this deco chose to alternate the pages to flip from side to side for added interest.

Knock, knock

Doors and windows can be added to the smallest of pages.

About the Author

Madeline Arendt describes herself as a self-taught artist. The only formal art classes she had were during her years in high school. Her desire to create began when she was a little girl. She was surrounded by creative people, with grandparents, parents, siblings, and other relatives who all worked in some way with creating handcrafted items. Being the youngest of three and the only girl in her immediate family, Madeline was exposed to sewing, embroidery, and cross-stitching as a young child. Before starting high school, she taught herself to knit and crochet. Because of her petite size, it was difficult to find stylish clothes that fit. She therefore had to sew most of her own clothes.

Being creative is a gift that she has used over and again in her life. It continued after marrying her high school sweetheart and raising a family of three children. Her sons and daughter grew up with a mother who loved decorating and redecorating their rooms. They always had cool, handmade costumes each Halloween. As years passed, Madeline acquired a reputation among her family and friends and they began to refer to her as "Martha," not Madeline. They called on her to help with decorating, to sew, to stencil, and to design and make invitations and favors for parties, showers, and weddings. She enjoyed the process of coming up with new and different ideas each time.

Madeline says she truly loves creating new designs and working with a variety of mediums. She finds it a challenge to look for new ways to combine the mediums, but it is one she enjoys. Madeline continues taking classes when and where she can to learn new things. She also teaches from time to time. Her belief is that you can never learn enough.

Acknowledgments

The following companies generously provided product used in the creation of the projects in this book:

Beacon Adhesives
125 MacQuesten Parkway South
Mount Vernon, New York 10550
www.beaconcreates.com

Krylon
101 Prospect Avenue NW
Cleveland, Ohio 44115-1093
www.krylon.com

Plaid Enterprises, Inc.
1301 River Forest Cove
Round Rock, Texas 78664
www.plaidonline.com

Ranger
15 Park Road
Tinton Falls, New Jersey 07724
www.rangerink.com

ThermOWeb
770 Glenn Avenue
Wheeling, Illinois 60090
www.thermoweb.com

Dedication

This book is dedicated firstly to my husband and children for being my biggest fans and always supporting my creative journey. To "the girls," for their friendship and cheerleading, and to a wonderful group of encouraging and supportive friends. Lastly, but not least, in memory of my dear sweet mother, who planted the seed of creativity.

Metric Equivalency Charts

mm-millimetres   cm-centimetres
inches to millimetres and centimetres

inches	mm	cm	inches	cm	inches	cm
⅛	3	0.3	9	22.9	30	76.2
¼	6	0.6	10	25.4	31	78.7
⅜	10	1.0	11	27.9	32	81.3
½	13	1.3	12	30.5	33	83.8
⅝	16	1.6	13	33.0	34	86.4
¾	19	1.9	14	35.6	35	88.9
⅞	22	2.2	15	38.1	36	91.4
1	25	2.5	16	40.6	37	94.0
1¼	32	3.2	17	43.2	38	96.5
1½	38	3.8	18	45.7	39	99.1
1¾	44	4.4	19	48.3	40	101.6
2	51	5.1	20	50.8	41	104.1
2½	64	6.4	21	53.3	42	106.7
3	76	7.6	22	55.9	43	109.2
3½	89	8.9	23	58.4	44	111.8
4	102	10.2	24	61.0	45	114.3
4½	114	11.4	25	63.5	46	116.8
5	127	12.7	26	66.0	47	119.4
6	152	15.2	27	68.6	48	121.9
7	178	17.8	28	71.1	49	124.5
8	203	20.3	29	73.7	50	127.0

yards to metres

yards	metres	yards	metres	yards	metres	yards	metres	yards	metres
⅛	0.11	2⅛	1.94	4⅛	3.77	6⅛	5.60	8⅛	7.43
¼	0.23	2¼	2.06	4¼	3.89	6¼	5.72	8¼	7.54
⅜	0.34	2⅜	2.17	4⅜	4.00	6⅜	5.83	8⅜	7.66
½	0.46	2½	2.29	4½	4.11	6½	5.94	8½	7.77
⅝	0.57	2⅝	2.40	4⅝	4.23	6⅝	6.06	8⅝	7.89
¾	0.69	2¾	2.51	4¾	4.34	6¾	6.17	8¾	8.00
⅞	0.80	2⅞	2.63	4⅞	4.46	6⅞	6.29	8⅞	8.12
1	0.91	3	2.74	5	4.57	7	6.40	9	8.23
1⅛	1.03	3⅛	2.86	5⅛	4.69	7⅛	6.52	9⅛	8.34
1¼	1.14	3¼	2.97	5¼	4.80	7¼	6.63	9¼	8.46
1⅜	1.26	3⅜	3.09	5⅜	4.91	7⅜	6.74	9⅜	8.57
1½	1.37	3½	3.20	5½	5.03	7½	6.86	9½	8.69
1⅝	1.49	3⅝	3.31	5⅝	5.14	7⅝	6.97	9⅝	8.80
1¾	1.60	3¾	3.43	5¾	5.26	7¾	7.09	9¾	8.92
1⅞	1.71	3⅞	3.54	5⅞	5.37	7⅞	7.20	9⅞	9.03
2	1.83	4	3.66	6	5.49	8	7.32	10	9.14

Index

19.95